POSH
NOSH

POSH NOSH

COLLINS & BROWN

The Good Housekeeping website is
www.goodhousekeeping.co.uk

ISBN 978-1-909397-00-2

A catalogue record for this book is available from
the British Library.

Reproduction by Dot Gradations Ltd, UK
Printed and bound by
1010 Printing International Ltd, China

This book can be ordered direct from the publisher.
Contact the marketing department, but try your
bookshop first.

www.anovabooks.com

NOTES

Both metric and imperial measures are given for
the recipes. Follow either set of measures, not a
mixture of both, as they are not interchangeable.

All spoon measures are level.
1 tsp = 5ml spoon; 1 tbsp = 15ml spoon.

Ovens and grills must be preheated to the specified
temperature.

Medium eggs should be used except where
otherwise specified. Free-range eggs are
recommended.

Note that some recipes contain raw or lightly
cooked eggs. The young, elderly, pregnant women
and anyone with an immune-deficiency disease
should avoid these because of the slight risk
of salmonella.

Contents

Cocktail O'clock

Easy Ways to Plan a Party

**Plan ahead and you are more likely to enjoy the occasion.
Avoid planning a meal that is too complicated, and don't tackle
a recipe that is totally unfamiliar – or have a practice run first.**

When deciding on a menu, keep it as well balanced as possible. Think about the colours, flavours and textures of the foods – rich and light, sweet and savoury, crunchy and smooth, hot and cold. Don't have cream or fruit featuring in all the courses; avoid an all-brown menu.

Select produce in season, for the best flavour and value for money. Check whether any of your guests have special dietary needs and plan appropriately. Try to cook an entirely meatless meal even if there is going to be just one vegetarian – it's not as difficult as it sounds, and rarely does anybody notice!

It is worthwhile choosing dishes that can be prepared well ahead of time or prepared up to a certain point, only needing a little last-minute finishing in the kitchen.

Getting started

Make a master shopping list and separate lists of dishes to be prepared ahead, with a note of when to make them. Plan fridge and freezer space; for a large party, you may need to make different arrangements such as asking your neighbour to keep some foods in their fridge, or putting bulky items into cool boxes. Check that you have candles if you plan to use them.

Make invitations to a dinner party over the phone about 10–12 days in advance. Mention whether it's a formal or informal occasion, the date and time, address if necessary, and say if there are any special dress requirements to avoid embarrassing situations! If you are sending written invitations, post them two to three weeks in advance.

Check that table linen is laundered and ironed in advance, and that you have clean glasses and cutlery. Clean the house a day or two beforehand. Buy or order wine and drinks in advance and avoid doing all the shopping at once.

Handy hints for entertaining

- Try to strike a balance between hot and cold items, light and substantial ones.
- Most supermarkets have a good selection of ready-to-eat or cook appetisers, if you haven't time to make some. You can also use good-quality bought ingredients, such as mayonnaise and fresh sauces, to save time.
- A freezer is invaluable when entertaining whether on a grand scale or just dinner for two.
- Keep a supply of ready-to-bake bread in the fridge or freezer for quick fresh bread. Freeze packs of half-baked breads to pop in the oven as and when needed.
- Keep a supply of luxury ice cream in the freezer.
- Remember to unwrap cheeses and bring them to room temperature at least an hour before serving, keeping them lightly covered, to prevent drying out, until the last minute.
- Make ice well in advance.
- During the winter, if you run out of fridge space, use a greenhouse or garage to keep drinks and other perishables cold.
- Use the microwave to reheat pre-cooked vegetables, sauces and gravy.
- Decide in advance where you are going to stack dirty plates. A kitchen overflowing with washing-up looks unsightly, so consider paying someone to do this for you on the day.

Lemon and Rosemary Olives

To serve six, you will need:
a few fresh rosemary sprigs, plus
extra to garnish, 1 garlic clove,
175g (6oz) mixed black and green
Greek olives, pared zest of 1 lemon,
2 tbsp vodka (optional), 300ml
(½ pint) extra virgin olive oil.

1 Put the rosemary and garlic in a
   small heatproof bowl and pour
   over enough boiling water to
   cover. Leave for 1–2 minutes,
   then drain well.
2 Put the olives, lemon zest and
   vodka, if you like, in a glass jar
   and add the rosemary and garlic.
   Pour over enough oil to cover the
   olives. Cover and chill for at least
   24 hours before using.
3 To serve, remove the olives from
   the oil and garnish with sprigs
   of fresh rosemary. Use within
   one week.

SAVE MONEY

Don't waste the flavoured oil left
over from the olives. It's perfect
for using in marinades as well as
salad dressings.

Black Olive Bread

To make two loaves, you will need:
2 tsp traditional dried yeast, 500g
(1lb 2oz) strong white bread flour,
plus extra to dust, 2 tsp coarse salt,
plus extra to sprinkle, 6 tbsp extra
virgin olive oil, plus extra to grease,
100g (3½oz) black olives, pitted
and chopped.

1 Put 150ml (¼ pint) hand-hot water
   into a jug, stir in the yeast and
   leave for 10 minutes or until frothy.
   Put the flour into a bowl or a food
   processor, then add the salt, yeast
   mix, 200ml (7fl oz) warm water
   and 2 tbsp oil. Using a wooden
   spoon or the dough hook, mix
   for 2–3 minutes to make a soft,
   smooth dough. Put the dough
   into a lightly oiled bowl, cover
   with oiled clingfilm and leave in
   a warm place for 45 minutes or
   until doubled in size.

2 Punch the dough to knock out
   the air, then knead on a lightly
   floured worksurface for 1 minute.
   Add the olives and knead until
   combined. Divide in half, shape
   into rectangles and put into two
   greased tins, each about 25.5
   × 15cm (10 × 6in). Cover with
   clingfilm and leave in a warm
   place for 1 hour or until the dough
   is puffy.

3 Preheat the oven to 200°C (180°C
   fan oven) mark 6. Press your
   finger into the dough 12 times,
   drizzle 2 tbsp oil over the surface
   and sprinkle with salt. Bake for
   30–35 minutes until golden.
   Drizzle with the remaining oil.
   Slice and serve warm.

Tapenade

To serve four, you will need:
3 tbsp capers, rinsed and drained,
75g (3oz) pitted black olives, 50g can
anchovy fillets in oil, drained, 100ml
(3½fl oz) olive oil, 2 tbsp brandy,
freshly ground black pepper,
vegetable sticks or grilled vegetables
or toasted French bread to serve.

1 Put the capers into a blender or
   food processor with the olives and
   anchovies. Process briefly to chop.
2 With the motor running, add the
   oil in a steady stream. Stir in the
   brandy and season with ground
   black pepper to taste. Transfer to
   a serving bowl.
3 Serve the tapenade with a
   selection of raw vegetable sticks,
   grilled vegetables or toasted
   French bread.

Houmous

To serve six, you will need:
400g can chickpeas, drained and
rinsed, juice of 1 lemon, 4 tbsp tahini,
1 garlic clove, crushed, 5 tbsp extra
virgin olive oil, salt and freshly
ground black pepper, warm pitta
bread or toasted flatbreads to serve.

1 Put the chickpeas, lemon juice,
   tahini, garlic and oil in a blender
   or food processor. Season
   generously with salt and ground
   black pepper, then whiz to a paste.
2 Spoon the houmous into a bowl,
   then cover and chill until needed.
3 Serve with warm pitta bread or
   toasted flatbreads.

Black Olive Houmous

Stir 25g (1oz) roughly chopped pitted
black olives and 1 tsp paprika into
the houmous paste. Sprinkle with
a little extra paprika and oil, if you
like. Serve with bread sticks and raw
carrot sticks.

Scotch Quail Eggs

Hands-on time: 25 minutes
Cooking time: about 20 minutes

300g (11oz) Cumberland pork sausages, about 5

flour to dust

1 large egg, lightly beaten

75g (3oz) dried breadcrumbs

12 hard-boiled quail eggs

2–3 tbsp vegetable oil to fry

sea salt and mustard to serve

SAVE EFFORT

For ease, buy pre-cooked and peeled quail eggs. Alternatively, hard-boil your own in simmering water for 3–4 minutes up to two days ahead, then cool, peel, cover and chill. Complete the recipe up to one day ahead (if needed). Cool and chill. Allow to come up to room temperature, or warm in a 180°C (160°C fan oven) mark 4 oven for 5–10 minutes, before serving.

1 Preheat the oven to 200°C (180°C fan oven) mark 6. Squeeze the sausage meat out of the skins into a bowl and discard the skins. Put some flour, the egg and breadcrumbs into separate small bowls.

2 Divide the meat into 12 equal portions. With lightly floured hands, form a portion into a flat patty about 6.5cm (2½in) across in the palm of one hand. Put a boiled quail egg in the middle, then shape the meat around it. Put to one side on a board and repeat with the remaining eggs and meat.

3 Dip the covered eggs in flour, tap off excess, then dip in the beaten egg, and coat in the breadcrumbs.

4 Heat the oil in a large frying pan over a medium-high heat. Add the coated eggs and fry, turning regularly, until golden on each side (in batches if necessary). Transfer to a baking tray.

5 Cook the eggs in the oven for 10 minutes. Serve warm or at room temperature with salt and mustard.

Mini Eggs Benedict

Hands-on time: 20 minutes
Cooking time: about 5 minutes

oil to grease
12 quail eggs
3 standard thin-cut white bread slices
1 tbsp mayonnaise or
    ready-made hollandaise
2–3 ham slices
freshly ground black pepper

SAVE EFFORT

These are best made fresh, but
will sit happily for 30 minutes
once assembled.

1 Bring a medium pan quarter-filled
   with water to a simmer. Grease a
   lipped baking tray, then put the tray
   on top of the pan to heat up. Carefully
   crack all the quail eggs into a bowl,
   then gently pour the eggs on to the
   hot tray, moving the yolks so they are
   not touching one another. The steam
   will cook the eggs in 3–5 minutes.

2 Meanwhile, toast the bread slices.
   Use a 3.5cm (1½in) round cutter to
   stamp out 12 circles of toast. Top each
   circle with a dab of mayonnaise or
   hollandaise. Next, stamp out ham
   circles with the same cutter and put
   one circle on each toast stack.

3 When the egg whites are cooked (and
   the yolks are still soft), lift the tray
   off the steam. Use the cutter to stamp
   around each yolk and use a palette
   knife to transfer the egg circles to the
   stacks. Crack over some black pepper
   and serve.

Avocado Scoops

🍴 **Hands-on time:** 15 minutes

2 ripe avocados

½ red onion, finely chopped

1 tomato, seeded and finely chopped

juice of 1 lime

few drops of Tabasco, to taste

a small handful of fresh coriander, chopped, plus extra to garnish

200g bag lightly salted tortilla chips

salt and freshly ground black pepper

1 Halve, stone and peel the avocados. Finely chop the flesh then add to a bowl. Stir through the onion, tomato, lime juice, Tabasco, coriander and some seasoning.

2 Spoon the mixture on to each tortila chip and sprinkle with chopped coriander. Serve.

SAVE EFFORT

Make the avocado mixture up to 3 hours ahead but don't add the coriander. Cover and chill. Complete the recipe to serve up to 30 minutes in advance.

Makes about 30

Take 5 Perfect Dips

Tzatziki

To serve eight, you will need:
1 cucumber, 300g (11oz) Greek-style yogurt, 2 tsp olive oil, 2 tbsp freshly chopped mint, 1 large garlic clove, crushed, salt and freshly ground black pepper, warm pitta bread and vegetable sticks to serve.

1 Halve, seed and dice the cucumber and put into a bowl.
2 Add the yogurt and oil. Stir in the mint and garlic, and season to taste. Cover and chill in the fridge until ready to serve.
3 Serve with warm pitta bread and vegetable sticks.

Blue Cheese Dip

To serve six, you will need:
150ml (¼ pint) soured cream, 1 garlic clove, crushed, 175g (6oz) blue Stilton, juice of 1 lemon, salt and freshly ground black pepper, snipped chives to garnish, vegetable sticks to serve.

1 Put all the ingredients into a blender or food processor and work to a smooth paste.
2 Transfer to a serving dish and chill until required. Check the seasoning, sprinkle with chives and serve with a selection of raw vegetable sticks.

Red Pepper and Feta Dip

To make about 375g (13oz) (25 tbsp), you will need:
290g jar roasted red peppers, drained, 200g (7oz) feta, crumbled, 1 small garlic clove, 1 tbsp natural yogurt, toasted pitta bread to serve.

1 Put all the ingredients into a blender or food processor and whiz until smooth. Serve the dip with strips of toasted pitta bread.

Taramasalata

To serve six, you will need:
100g (3½oz) country-style bread, crusts removed, 75g (3oz) smoked cod roe, 2 tbsp lemon juice, 100ml (3½fl oz) light olive oil, freshly ground black pepper, warm pitta bread or toasted flatbreads to serve.

1 Put the bread into a bowl, cover with cold water and leave to soak for 10 minutes. Drain and squeeze out most of the water.
2 Soak the smoked cod roe in cold water to cover for 10 minutes, then drain and remove the skin.
3 Put the roe in a blender or food processor with the bread and whiz for 30 seconds. With the motor running, add the lemon juice and oil, and whiz briefly to combine. Season with ground black pepper to taste.
4 Spoon into a bowl, cover and chill until needed. Serve with warm pitta bread or toasted flatbreads.

Guacamole

To serve six, you will need:
2 ripe avocados, 2 small tomatoes, seeded and chopped, juice of 2 limes, 2 tbsp extra virgin olive oil, 2 tbsp freshly chopped coriander, salt and freshly ground black pepper, tortilla chips, or warm pitta bread and vegetable sticks to serve.

1 Cut the avocados in half, remove the stones and peel away the skin. Tip the flesh into a bowl and mash with a fork.
2 Quickly add the tomatoes, lime juice, oil and chopped coriander. Mix well and season with salt and ground black pepper to taste. Cover and chill in the fridge until ready to serve.
3 Serve the guacamole with tortilla chips or warm pitta bread and vegetable sticks.

Sweet Onion Sausage Rolls

Hands-on time: 20 minutes, plus chilling
Cooking time: about 15 minutes

300g (11oz) sausage meat

a small handful of fresh parsley,
    finely chopped

375g pack ready-rolled shortcrust pastry
    (in a rectangular sheet)

2 tbsp onion marmalade (bought)

1 large egg, lightly beaten

poppy seeds to sprinkle

1 Put the sausage meat into a large
   bowl; stir in the parsley. Unroll the
   pastry sheet and cut lengthways into
   four equal strips. Thinly spread 1 tbsp
   of the onion marmalade lengthways
   down the middle of one of the strips.
   Repeat with one other strip.

2 Divide the sausage mixture in half.
   Shape one half into a thin cylinder as
   long as the pastry strips, then position
   it on top of one of the marmalade
   strips. Repeat with remaining sausage
   mixture. Brush the visible pastry
   around the sausage cylinders with
   beaten egg, then top with remaining
   pastry strips. Press down on the edges

to seal. Transfer to a baking sheet
and chill for 30 minutes.

3 Preheat the oven to 200°C (180°C
   fan oven) mark 6. Line two baking
   trays with baking parchment. Brush
   both rolls with egg and sprinkle
   over some poppy seeds. Cut into
   4cm (1½in) pieces and place on the
   prepared trays. Cook for 15 minutes or
   until golden. Serve warm or at room
   temperature.

SAVE TIME

Complete up to the end of step 2
up to a day ahead. Cover and chill.
Complete the recipe to serve.
If you can't find sausage meat,
then simply peel the skins off
your favourite pork sausages.

Makes about 22

Cheese and Bacon Puffs

Hands-on time: 20 minutes
Cooking time: about 20 minutes

75g (3oz) finely chopped streaky bacon

75g (3oz) unsalted butter

75ml (3fl oz) each milk and water

½ tsp English mustard powder

½ tsp paprika

75g (3oz) plain flour

2 large eggs

25g (1oz) Parmesan, grated, plus extra
for sprinkling

a large handful of finely chopped fresh
curly parsley

salt and freshly ground black pepper

1 Cook the bacon in a pan until crisp
   and put to one side.

2 In a large pan, heat the butter, milk
   and water, mustard powder, paprika
   and some seasoning. When the
   mixture comes to the boil, take off
   the heat and stir in the flour. Stir for 2
   minutes until the mixture comes away
   from the sides of the pan. Transfer to a
   bowl and leave to cool.

3 Preheat the oven to 200°C (180°C fan
   oven) mark 6. Gradually beat up to 2
   eggs into the flour mixture to give it a
   dropping consistency – it should fall
   off the spoon reluctantly. Save any of
   the remaining egg.

4 Stir the Parmesan, parsley and the
   reserved bacon into the flour mixture.
   Dollop teaspoonfuls on to baking
   sheets, spacing well apart. Brush with
   the remaining egg and sprinkle with
   a little grated Parmesan. Cook in the
   oven for 10–12 minutes until golden
   and puffed. Serve immediately.

FREEZE AHEAD

Freeze finished, uncooked balls on
a baking sheet lined with baking
parchment. When solid, pack into
an airtight container and freeze for
up to one month. To serve, cook
from frozen for 15–20 minutes.

Makes 24

Thai Crab Mayo Croustades

Hands-on time: 15 minutes

100g (3½oz) white crab meat

1½ tsp fish sauce

2½ tbsp mayonnaise

½–1 red chilli, seeded and
  finely chopped (see Safety Tip)

a small handful of fresh coriander,
  chopped, plus extra to garnish

15 mini croustade cases

salt and freshly ground black pepper

SAVE TIME

Make the crab mixture up to a day
ahead but don't add the coriander.
Cover and chill. Complete the
recipe to serve.

1 In a medium bowl, stir together
the first five ingredients. Check the
seasoning and adjust to taste. Fill each
croustade case with a spoonful of the
crab mixture, then garnish with extra
coriander, if you like.

SAFETY TIP

· Chillies vary enormously in
  strength, from quite mild to
  blisteringly hot, depending on
  the type of chilli and its ripeness.
  Taste a small piece first to check
  it's not too hot for you.

· Be extremely careful when
  handling chillies not to touch or
  rub your eyes with your fingers,
  as they will sting. Wash knives
  immediately after handling
  chillies for the same reason. As
  a precaution, use rubber gloves
  when preparing them, if you like.

Smoked Salmon Blinis

TAKE 5

 Hands-on time: 5 minutes

3 tbsp crème fraîche

16 small blinis or 125g pack

125g (4oz) thinly sliced smoked salmon

1 tbsp freshly snipped chives

lemon wedges to serve

1 Spread the crème fraîche on to the blinis, then fold the salmon loosely on top. Sprinkle with chives and serve with lemon wedges to squeeze over.

SAVE TIME

If you can't find blinis, you can use small pieces of pumpernickel or rye bread.

SAVE EFFORT

Instead of smoked salmon, use hot-smoked salmon flakes. Put the salmon flakes, crème fraîche and a little ground black pepper into a bowl and mix gently. Put 1 tsp of the mixture on to each blini, sprinkle with chopped chives and serve immediately.

Makes 16

Mango Chicken Skewers
with Basil Raita

Hands-on time: 15 minutes
Cooking time: about 10 minutes

3 × 125g (4oz) skinless chicken breasts,
   cut into bite-size pieces

3 tbsp mango chutney

1 tsp vegetable oil

finely grated zest and juice of 1 lemon

150g (5oz) natural yogurt

¼ cucumber, grated

a small handful of basil leaves,
   finely sliced, plus extra small leaves
   to garnish

salt and freshly ground black pepper

1 Put the chicken pieces into a bowl
   with the mango chutney, oil, plenty of
   seasoning and half each of the
   lemon zest and juice.

2 Heat a griddle pan to high and cook
   the chicken for about 6–8 minutes,
   turning occasionally, until cooked
   through and lightly charred.

3 Meanwhile, make the raita. In a small
   serving bowl, stir together the yogurt,
   cucumber, remaining lemon zest and
   juice and sliced basil. Season well.

4 When the chicken is cooked, top
   each piece with a small basil leaf and
   secure in place with a cocktail stick.
   Serve with the raita.

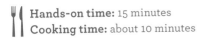
SAVE TIME

Cook the chicken and make the
raita up to a day ahead, but don't
add basil. Cover and chill. To serve,
allow chicken to come to room
temperature; complete the recipe.

Makes about 18

Cranberry Crush

Hands-on time: 5 minutes

75cl bottle sparkling wine, such as
  cava, chilled
300ml (½ pint) Calvados
1 litre (1¾ pints) cranberry juice, chilled
450ml (¾ pint) sparkling water, chilled
1 small orange, thinly sliced into rounds
10–12 ice cubes

1 Pour the sparkling wine, Calvados and cranberry juice into a large glass serving bowl.
2 Just before serving, pour in the sparkling water, stir, then add the orange slices and 10–12 ice cubes. Ladle into glasses and serve immediately.

HEALTHY TIP

For an alternative flavour, use pomegranate juice instead of cranberry, and add a spoonful of fresh pomegranate seeds to each glass instead of orange slices.

Makes 12

Whisky Refresher

Hands-on time: 5 minutes

100ml (3½fl oz) whisky or bourbon
500ml (17fl oz) lemonade
4 fresh mint sprigs
1 lime, cut into 4 wedges

1 Fill four tumblers with crushed ice. Pour a quarter each of the whisky or bourbon and lemonade into each glass. Garnish with mint sprigs and lime wedges. Serve immediately.

Serves 4

Champagne Cocktail

🍴 **Hands-on time:** 5 minutes

125ml (4fl oz) Grand Marnier

75ml (2½fl oz) grenadine

1 large orange, cut into 8 wedges

8 sugar cubes or sugar sticks

75cl bottle champagne, cava or other sparkling wine, chilled

1 Measure out the Grand Marnier and grenadine and divide among eight champagne glasses. Add an orange wedge and a sugar cube or stick to each glass.

2 Top up the glasses with the champagne, cava or sparkling wine and serve immediately.

SAVE EFFORT

For a simple way to get a **Classic Champagne Cocktail**: put a sugar cube in each glass, add 2 drops Angostura bitters and 2 tsp brandy. Top up with chilled champagne.

Serves 8

Take 5 Classic Cocktails

Alcoholic drinks and vegetarians

Animal-derived ingredients, such as gelatine (from cattle) and isinglass (from fish) are often used as fining agents in wine, sherry, port, beer and cider. For this reason some vegetarians prefer to drink only vegetarian alternatives. You can find these in supermarkets and online. Spirits (apart from some malt whiskies, which have been matured in sherry casks) and many liqueurs are generally acceptable to vegetarians.

Whisky Sour

To serve one you will need:
juice of ½ lemon, 1 tsp sugar, 25ml (1fl oz) rye whisky and crushed ice.

1 Mix together the lemon juice, sugar and whisky, and shake well with the ice.
2 Serve in a whisky tumbler.

Buck's Fizz

To serve one you will need:
juice from 1 small orange, 150ml (¼ pint) champagne.

1 Strain the orange juice into a champagne flute and top up with chilled champagne. Serve at once.

Piña Colada

To serve one you will need:
85ml (3fl oz) white rum, 125ml (4fl oz) pineapple juice, 50ml (2fl oz) coconut cream, crushed ice, 1 pineapple slice and 1 cherry to garnish.

1   Blend together the rum, pineapple juice, coconut cream and the crushed ice.
2   Pour into a large goblet or a hollowed-out pineapple half.
3   Garnish with a slice of pineapple and a cherry. Serve with straws.

Daiquiri

To serve one you will need:
juice of ½ lime or ¼ lemon, 1 tsp sugar, 25ml (1fl oz) white rum, crushed ice, extra fruit juice and caster sugar to frost.

1   Mix the fruit juice, sugar and rum and shake well with the crushed ice in a shaker.
2   Dip the edges of the glass in a little more fruit juice and then into caster sugar to frost the rim before filling.

Margarita

To serve one you will need:
lemon juice, 125ml (4fl oz) tequila, 25ml (1fl oz) curaçao and 25ml (1fl oz) lemon or lime juice, salt.

1   Dip the edges of a chilled glass into lemon or lime juice and then salt.
2   In a shaker, mix the tequila, curaçao and lemon or lime juice.
3   Strain into the chilled glass and serve immediately.

Elderflower Cordial

To make about 1.1 litres (2 pints)
you will need:
2kg (4½lb) golden granulated sugar,
80g (just over 3oz) citric acid,
2 medium lemons, sliced, 20 large
young elderflower heads (shake to
release any insects).

1 Bring 1.1 litres (2 pints) water to
   the boil, add the sugar and stir
   until dissolved.
2 Add the citric acid and lemon
   slices. Stir in the flower heads.
   Leave overnight, covered.
3 In the morning sieve. If you want
   it clearer, strain again through a
   piece of muslin or a coffee filter.
   Bottle, give some away and keep
   the rest in the fridge – it will last
   for months!

Warming Ginger Soda

To serve six, you will need:
300g (11oz) unpeeled fresh root
ginger, finely sliced, 225g (8oz) caster
sugar, grated zest and juice of 1½
lemons, 1 litre (1¾ pints) soda water.

1 Put the root ginger into a pan
   with the sugar and lemon zest and
   juice. Add about 600ml (1 pint)
   cold water to cover. Heat gently to
   dissolve the sugar, then turn up
   the heat and simmer gently for
   10 minutes.
2 Strain through a fine sieve into
   a jug. Leave to cool for at least
   10 minutes, then top up with
   soda water.

SAVE TIME

Make the ginger syrup up to three
days ahead. Chill. Add soda to serve.

'Still' Lemonade

To make about 1.1 litres (2 pints),
you will need:
3 lemons, 175g (6oz) sugar.

1 Remove the lemon zest thinly with
a potato peeler.
2 Put the zest and sugar into a bowl
or large jug and pour on 900ml
(1½ pints) boiling water. Cover and
leave to cool, stirring occasionally.
3 Add the juice of the lemons and
strain the lemonade. Serve chilled.

Cranberry Cooler

To serve one you will need:
ice cubes, 75ml (2½fl oz) cranberry
juice, lemonade or sparkling water,
chilled, 1 lemon slice to serve.

1 Half-fill a tall glass with ice and
pour in the cranberry juice.
2 Top up with lemonade. If you'd
prefer the drink to be less sweet,
double the amount of cranberry
juice and top up with sparkling
water. Stir well and serve with a
slice of lemon.

Fruity Carrot with Ginger

To serve 400ml (14fl oz) you
will need:
2 medium oranges, 1cm (½in) piece
fresh root ginger, peeled and roughly
chopped, 150ml (¼ pint) freshly
pressed apple juice or 2 dessert
apples, juiced, 150ml (¼ pint) freshly
pressed carrot juice or 3 medium
carrots, 250g (9oz), juiced, fresh mint
leaves to decorate.

1 Using a sharp knife, cut a slice of
orange and put to one side for the
decoration. Cut off the peel from
the oranges, removing as much of
the white pith as possible. Chop
the flesh roughly, discarding any
pips, and put into a blender. Add
the chopped ginger.
2 Pour in the apple and carrot juice
and blend until smooth. Divide
between two glasses, decorate
with the quartered orange slices
and a mint leaf and serve.

Elderflower Fizz

about 200ml (7fl oz) cloudy apple juice
100ml (4fl oz) elderflower liqueur
chilled sparkling white or rosé wine
apple slices and fresh mint sprigs
   to garnish

1 Half-fill four champagne flutes with
  the cloudy apple juice, then add a
  quarter of elderflower liqueur to
  each glass and top up with chilled
  sparkling wine.
2 Garnish with a slice of apple and
  a sprig of mint.

HEALTHY TIP

For a thirst-quenching non-alcoholic
elderflower fizz, just replace the
wine with chilled sparkling water.

Serves 4

Tangerine Jelly Shots

Hands-on time: 10 minutes, plus chilling
Cooking time: about 3 minutes

5 gelatine leaves

12 tangerines, about 1kg (2lb 2oz)

150g (5oz) caster sugar

double cream, to serve (optional)

SAVE EFFORT

Make these delicious jellies up to two days ahead.

1 Put the gelatine in a bowl and cover with cold water. Leave to soak for 5 minutes. Meanwhile zest 2 tangerines and put the zest into a large pan. Squeeze the juice from the zested and whole tangerines and add to the pan with the sugar.

2 Lift the gelatine out of the water (discard the water) and add to the pan. Heat gently until the sugar dissolves. Strain the mixture into a large jug with a good pouring spout and make up to 1 litre (1¾ pints) with cold water. Pour the mixture into 12 small glasses and chill in the fridge for at least 5 hours, preferably overnight.

3 To serve, take the jellies out of fridge 5 minutes before you need them to allow to soften slightly. Serve with spoons and topped with double cream, if you like.

Makes 12

Oysters with Three Sauces

Purists may eat oysters with just lemon and Tabasco, but here are three alternative sauces that marry well with this luxury starter.

Allow 4–6 oysters per person, and make sure they are as fresh as can be. Shucking them at home is ideal – alternatively, ask your fishmonger to do it for you. Serve on a large platter of crushed ice or rock salt.

Shallot Vinegar

Also known as mignonette sauce, this is a real classic to serve with oysters. The sharpness of the vinegar cuts through the richness of the shellfish.

Hands-on time: 5 minutes, plus infusing
Makes enough to dress up to 24 oysters

2 finely chopped shallots
100ml (3½fl oz) red wine vinegar
1½ tbsp caster sugar

1 In a small bowl, stir together the shallots, red wine vinegar and caster sugar. Stir and leave to infuse for 1 hour. Empty into a serving bowl.

SAVE EFFORT

Prepare up to a day ahead. Cover and chill. Allow to come up to room temperature before serving.

Zesty Chilli Sauce

Hands-on time: 5 minutes
Makes enough to dress up to 24 oysters

125g (4oz) sweet chilli sauce
2 tbsp extra virgin olive oil
grated zest and juice of 2 limes
2 tbsp freshly chopped coriander
salt and freshly ground black pepper

1 In a small bowl, stir together the sweet chilli sauce, oil, lime zest and juice, coriander and some seasoning. Empty into a serving bowl.

Oriental Drizzle

Hands-on time: 5 minutes
Makes enough to dress up to 24 oysters

2 tbsp sesame oil
4 tbsp soy sauce
1 tsp finely grated fresh root ginger
juice of ½ lemon
1 finely chopped small garlic clove
2 finely sliced spring onions
salt and freshly ground black pepper

1 In a small bowl, stir together the oil, soy sauce, ginger, lemon juice, garlic, spring onions and some seasoning. Empty into a serving bowl.

SAVE EFFORT

Prepare up to a day ahead, but don't add the coriander. Cover and chill. Allow to come up to room temperature before completing the recipe to serve.

SAVE EFFORT

Prepare up to a day ahead but don't add the spring onion. Cover and chill. To serve, allow to come up to room temperature before completing the recipe.

Bites, Brunches and Sides

Classic Houmous

Hands-on time: 5 minutes

400g can chickpeas

40ml (1½fl oz) olive oil, plus extra
   to drizzle

1½ tbsp lemon juice

1 small garlic clove

¼ tsp ground cumin

salt and freshly ground black pepper

sprinkle of paprika or cayenne pepper
   (optional)

breadsticks and toasted pitta bread
   to serve

1 Drain and rinse the chickpeas. Put a spoonful to one side then put the rest into a food processor with the oil, lemon juice, 1 tbsp water, garlic, ground cumin and plenty of seasoning. Whiz until smooth, then check the seasoning.

2 Scrape into a serving dish. Garnish with the reserved chickpeas, a sprinkle of paprika or cayenne pepper, if you like, and a drizzle of oil. Serve with breadsticks and toasted pitta bread for scooping.

SAVE TIME

Make up to a day ahead, but don't garnish. Drizzle a little oil over the reserved whole chickpeas; cover and chill in a bowl. Completethe recipe to serve.

Serves 6

Speedy Beetroot Dip

Hands-on time: 5 minutes

25g (1oz) Parmesan

500g (1lb 2oz) drained, vacuum-packed cooked beetroot

100g (3½oz) full-fat cream cheese

a small handful of fresh mint leaves, plus extra to garnish

salt and freshly ground black pepper

breadsticks and toasted pitta bread to serve

1 In a food processor, whiz the Parmesan until finely crumbed, then add the beetroot, cream cheese, mint leaves and plenty of seasoning. Whiz again until smooth and check the seasoning.

2 Transfer to a small serving bowl and garnish with a few mint leaves. Serve with breadsticks and toasted pittas.

SAVE TIME

Vacuum-packed beetroot makes an almost instant dip. Make up to one day ahead, but don't garnish. Cover and chill in a bowl. Complete the recipe to serve.

Serves 6

Pitta Bread

Hands-on time 20 minutes, plus rising
Cooking time: about 8 minutes per batch, plus cooling

15g (½oz) fresh yeast or
  1½ tsp traditional dried yeast and
  1 tsp sugar

700g (1½lb) strong white flour, plus extra
  to dust

1 tsp salt

1 tbsp caster sugar

1 tbsp olive oil, plus extra to grease

1 Blend the fresh yeast with 450ml (¾ pint) tepid water. If using dried yeast, sprinkle it into the water with the sugar and leave in a warm place for 15 minutes or until frothy.

2 Put the flour, salt and sugar into a bowl, make a well in the centre and pour in the yeast liquid with the oil. Mix to a smooth dough, then turn out on to a lightly floured worksurface and knead for 10 minutes or until smooth and elastic.

3 Place the dough in a large bowl, cover with oiled clingfilm and leave to rise in a warm place until doubled in size.

4 Divide the dough into 16 pieces and roll each into an oval shape about 20.5cm (8in) long. Place on floured baking sheets, cover with oiled clingfilm and leave in a warm place for about 30 minutes until slightly risen and puffy. Preheat the oven to 240°C (220°C fan oven) mark 9.

5 Bake the pittas in batches for 5–8 minutes only. They should be just lightly browned on top. Remove from the oven and wrap in a clean tea towel. Repeat with the remaining pittas.

6 When the pittas are warm enough to handle, but not completely cold, transfer them to a plastic bag and leave until cold. This will ensure that they have a soft crust.

7 To serve, warm in the oven, or toast lightly. Split and fill with salad, cheese, cold meats or your favourite sandwich filling. Or, cut into strips and serve with dips.

Makes 16 pitta breads

Perfect Eggs

Follow these tried and tested steps for poached, coddled and boiled eggs.

Poaching

1 Heat about 8cm (3¼in) of lightly salted water in a shallow frying pan to a bare simmer. Crack a very fresh egg into a cup, then slip it into the water. (The whites in a fresh egg are firmer and will form a 'nest' for the yolk while older egg whites are watery and spread out in the pan.)

2 Cook for 3–4 minutes until the white is barely set. Remove the egg with a slotted spoon and drain on kitchen paper.

Perfect coddling

1 Using a slotted spoon, gently lower the whole eggs into a pan of simmering water, then take the pan off the heat.

2 Leave the eggs to stand in the water for 4–5 minutes, where they will cook gently with the residual heat of the water.

2

Perfect boiled eggs

There are two ways to boil an egg: starting in boiling water or starting in cold water. Both work well as long as you follow certain rules:

- ❑ The egg must be at room temperature
- ❑ For both methods, cover the eggs with water, plus 2.5cm (1in) or so extra
- ❑ If starting in boiling water, use an 'egg pick', if you like, to pierce the broad end of the shell. This allows air in the pocket at the base of the egg to escape and avoids cracking
- ❑ Gently lower in the eggs using a long spoon to avoid cracking them
- ❑ Cook at a simmer rather than a rolling boil

Boiling: method 1

1. Bring a small pan of water to the boil. Once the water is boiling, add a medium egg. For a soft-boiled egg, cook for 6 minutes; for a salad egg, cook for 8 minutes; and for a hard-boiled egg, cook for 10 minutes.
2. Remove the egg from the water with a slotted spoon and serve.

Boiling: method 2

1. Put a medium egg in a small pan and cover with cold water. Put on a lid and bring to the boil. When the water begins to boil, remove the lid and cook for 2 minutes for a soft-boiled egg, 5 minutes for a salad egg, and 7 minutes for a

Duck Egg and Asparagus Dippers

Hands-on time: 15 minutes
Cooking time: about 6 minutes

600g (1lb 5oz) asparagus spears
   (not the fine variety)
6 duck eggs
extra virgin olive oil, to drizzle
salt and freshly ground black pepper
sourdough bread (optional) to serve

1 Holding both ends of an asparagus spear in your hands, bend gently until it snaps. Discard the woody end (or keep to make soups or stocks). Trim all the remaining spears to this length. Use a vegetable peeler to shave any knobbly or woody bits below the tip of each spear.

2 Divide the asparagus equally into six piles, then tie each neatly into a bundle with string.

3 Bring two medium pans of water to the boil. Add the eggs to one pan and simmer for exactly 5½ minutes. Add the asparagus bundles to the other pan and cook for 1 minute until just tender. Drain the asparagus and leave to steam-dry in the colander for 3 minutes. Drain the eggs.

4 Put one asparagus bundle on each plate, drizzle with a little extra virgin olive oil and season with salt and ground black pepper. Serve with the eggs, plus a slice of sourdough bread, if you like.

SAVE TIME

Prepare the asparagus to the end of step 2 up to 2 hours in advance. Chill the bundles, then complete the recipe to serve.

Eggs Benedict

Hands-on time: 15 minutes
Cooking time: 10 minutes

4 slices bread

4 medium eggs

150ml (¼ pint) hollandaise sauce

4 thin slices lean ham

fresh parsley sprigs to garnish

1 Toast the bread on both sides. Poach the eggs. Gently warm the hollandaise sauce.

2 Top each slice of toast with a folded slice of ham, then with a poached egg. Finally, coat the eggs with hollandaise sauce.

3 Garnish each with a sprig of parsley and serve.

SAVE EFFORT

For a delicious alternative recipe try **Eggs Florentine**:

Cook 900g (2lb) washed spinach in a pan with a little salt until tender. Drain well, chop and reheat with 15g (½oz) butter. Melt 25g (1oz) butter, stir in 3 tbsp plain flour and cook, stirring, until thickened. Add 50g (2oz) grated Gruyère or Cheddar and season. Do not allow to boil. Poach the eggs. Put the spinach into an ovenproof dish, arrange the eggs on top and pour the cheese sauce over them. Sprinkle with 25g (1oz) grated cheese and brown under the grill.

Serves 4

Perfect Scrambled Eggs

There are numerous ways to cook with eggs – from the simplest techniques such as boiling, poaching and scrambling, to more complex techniques such as making omelettes, soufflés and meringues. Follow these instructions for scrambled eggs with perfect results.

1. Allow 2 eggs per person. Break the eggs into a bowl, then beat well but lightly with a fork and season with salt and freshly ground black pepper.
2. Melt a knob of butter in a small heavy-based pan over a low heat – use a heat diffuser if necessary. (Using a non-stick pan minimises the amount of butter you need to use.)
3. Pour in the eggs and start stirring immediately, using a wooden spoon or a flat-headed spatula to break up the lumps as they form. Keep the eggs moving about as much as possible during cooking.

3

4

4 As the eggs start to set, scrape the bottom of the pan to keep the eggs from overcooking and to break up any larger lumps that may form. Your aim is to have a smooth mixture with no noticeable lumps.

5 Scrambled eggs may be well cooked and firm, or 'loose' and runny; this is a matter of taste. They will continue to cook when taken off the heat, so remove them when they are still softer than you want to serve them.

Microwave scrambled eggs

Put the eggs, milk, if you like, and the butter into a bowl and beat well. Microwave on full power (850W) for 1 minute (the mixture should be just starting to set around the edges), then beat again. Microwave again at full power for 2–3 minutes, stirring every 30 seconds, until the eggs are cooked the way you like them.

Scrambled Eggs with Smoked Salmon

Hands-on time: 10 minutes
Cooking time: 5 minutes

6 large eggs

25g (1oz) butter, plus extra to spread

100g (3½oz) mascarpone

125g pack smoked salmon, sliced,
  or smoked salmon trimmings

6 slices sourdough or rye bread, toasted,
  buttered and cut into slim rectangles
  for soldiers

salt and freshly ground black pepper

1 Crack the eggs into a jug and lightly beat together. Season well.

2 Melt the butter in a non-stick pan over a low heat. Add the eggs and stir constantly until the mixture thickens. Add the mascarpone and season well. Cook for 1–2 minutes longer, until the mixture just becomes firm, then fold in the smoked salmon. Serve at once with toasted bread soldiers.

Serves 4

Layered Omelette Cake

Hands-on time: 30 minutes, plus chilling
Cooking time: about 25 minutes, plus cooling

16 large eggs

5 tbsp freshly chopped chives

2 tbsp vegetable oil

500g (1lb 2oz) full-fat cream cheese

1 red pepper, seeded and finely diced

½ red chilli, seeded and finely chopped
   (see Safety Tip, page 26)

50g (2oz) watercress, chopped, plus extra
   to garnish

salt and freshly ground black pepper

1 Beat the eggs in a large jug with 2 tbsp
   of the chives and plenty of seasoning.
   Heat ½ tbsp of the oil in a 20.5cm
   (8in) non-stick frying pan and pour
   in a quarter of the egg mixture. Swirl
   the pan to ensure the base is covered.
   Using a spatula, occasionally push
   the mixture in from the sides of the
   pan while it's cooking (but ensuring
   the base is always fully covered with
   egg). Cook for 2–3 minutes until the
   underneath is golden, then flip the
   omelette and cook for a further 2–3

minutes. Transfer the omelette to a
plate to cool completely.

2 Repeat with the remaining oil and
   egg mixture to make three more
   omelettes (you may need to whisk the
   eggs before making each omelette to
   redistribute the chives).

3 While the omelettes are cooling, beat
   together the cream cheese, remaining
   chives, the red pepper, chilli, chopped
   watercress and some seasoning in a
   large bowl. Line a 20.5cm (8in) cake
   tin with clingfilm and place a cooled
   omelette in the base. Spread a third
   of the cream cheese mixture over the
   omelette. Repeat the stacking and
   spreading twice more and then top
   with the remaining omelette. Cover
   the tin with clingfilm and chill in the
   fridge for at least 30 minutes.

4 To serve, lift the omelette cake from
   the tin and peel off the clingfilm.
   Transfer to a serving plate or cake
   stand, garnish with watercress and
   serve in wedges.

Serves 12

Roast Baby Potatoes

Hands-on time: 3 minutes
Cooking time: about 35 minutes

1kg (2lb 2oz) baby potatoes
2 tbsp olive oil
salt and freshly ground black pepper

1 Preheat the oven to 220°C (200°C fan oven) mark 7. Empty the potatoes into a roasting tin and drizzle over the oil. Season well and toss gently to mix everything together.
2 Roast the potatoes for 30–35 minutes, tossing occasionally, until tender. Serve immediately.

SAVE EFFORT

Make to the end of step 1 up to 3 hours ahead. Cover and store at cool room temperature. Complete the recipe to serve.

Serves 6

Boulangère Potatoes

Hands-on time: 15 minutes
Cooking time: about 1½ hours

butter to grease

700g (1½lb) potatoes, unpeeled
and scrubbed

½ tbsp fresh thyme leaves

1 large sweet potato

500ml (17fl oz) vegetable stock

salt and freshly ground black pepper

1 Preheat the oven to 200°C (180°C fan oven) mark 6. Liberally grease a large, ovenproof casserole.

2 Slice the white potatoes as thinly as you can – a mandolin is good for this. Arrange half the slices in an even layer in the casserole, seasoning and sprinkling with some of the thyme as you go. Next, peel the sweet potato and slice as before. Arrange on top of the white potatoes in an even layer. Top with the remaining white potato slices, seasoning and sprinkling with the rest of the thyme.

3 Pour the stock into the casserole and press a sheet of buttered baking parchment on top of the potatoes. Cook for 1½ hours or until a knife can be easily pushed through the potatoes. Remove the baking parchment for the final 1 hour of cooking to allow the potatoes to brown. Serve.

FREEZE AHEAD

Complete the recipe up to three months ahead. Cool completely, then wrap the casserole in clingfilm and freeze. To serve, thaw completely, then preheat oven to 200°C (180°C fan oven) mark 6. Cover casserole with baking parchment and reheat for 30 minutes or until piping hot.

Spiced Red Cabbage

Hands-on time: 10 minutes
Cooking time: about 15 minutes

1 tbsp olive oil

15g (½oz) butter

½–1 tsp each ground ginger
and coriander

½ medium red cabbage, about
450g (1lb), finely shredded

2 tbsp balsamic vinegar

1 tbsp caster sugar

a large handful of fresh curly parsley,
roughly chopped

salt and freshly ground black pepper

1 Heat the oil and butter in a large pan
over a high heat. Stir in the spices and
cook for 1 minute. Add the cabbage
and cook for 10 minutes, stirring often,
until just softened.

2 Pour the vinegar over, add the sugar
and cook for 3 minutes. Stir in the
parsley and season to taste. Serve
immediately.

SAVE TIME

Red cabbage is traditionally
simmered for hours, but cooking it
quickly is a great alternative as it
retains a pleasing crunch. Make the
recipe without adding the parsley
up to 3 hours ahead. Cover and
chill. To serve, reheat gently in
pan and complete the recipe.

Serves 6

Thyme Tomatoes

Hands-on time: 3 minutes
Cooking time: about 12 minutes

500g (1lb 2oz) cherry tomatoes, on the vine

1 tbsp olive oil

3 fresh thyme sprigs

salt and freshly ground black pepper

1 Preheat the oven to 220°C (200°C fan oven) mark 7. Trim the tomatoes into small bunches and put the bunches into a small roasting tin. Drizzle over the oil and add the thyme. Season well with salt and ground black pepper.

2 Roast for 10–12 minutes until the tomatoes have burst but are still holding their shape. Remove the thyme and serve immediately.

SAVE EFFORT

Complete the recipe to the end of step 1 up to 3 hours in advance. Cover and store at a cool room temperature, then complete the recipe to serve.

Serves 6

Stir-fried Beans with Cherry Tomatoes

Hands-on time: 10 minutes
Cooking time: about 8 minutes

350g (12oz) green beans, trimmed

2 tsp olive oil

1 large garlic clove, crushed

150g (5oz) cherry or baby plum tomatoes, halved

2 tbsp freshly chopped flat-leafed parsley

salt and freshly ground black pepper

1 Cook the beans in salted boiling water for 4–5 minutes, then drain well.

2 Heat the oil in a wok or large frying pan over a high heat. Stir-fry the beans with the garlic and tomatoes for 2–3 minutes until the beans are tender and the tomatoes are just beginning to soften without losing their shape. Season well with salt and ground black pepper, then stir in the parsley and serve.

Serves 6

Succulent
Starters

Asparagus and Quail Egg Salad

Hands-on time: 20 minutes
Cooking time: 4 minutes

24 quail eggs

24 asparagus spears, trimmed

juice of ½ lemon

5 tbsp olive oil

4 large spring onions, finely sliced

100g (3½oz) watercress,
    roughly chopped

a few fresh dill and tarragon sprigs

salt and freshly ground black pepper

1 Gently lower the quail eggs into a pan of boiling water and cook for 2 minutes, then drain and plunge them into cold water. Cook the asparagus in salted boiling water for 2 minutes or until just tender. Drain, plunge into cold water and leave to cool.

2 Whisk together the lemon juice and oil and season with salt and ground black pepper. Stir in the spring onions and put to one side.

3 Shell the quail eggs and cut in half. Put into a large bowl with the asparagus, watercress, dill and tarragon sprigs. Pour the dressing over and lightly toss all the ingredients together. Adjust the seasoning and serve.

Serves 8

Melon and Chorizo Salad

Hands-on time: 10 minutes
Cooking time: about 8 minutes

1 cantaloupe melon

75ml (3fl oz) balsamic vinegar

1 tbsp runny honey

75g (3oz) chorizo, in one piece, skinned

1 tbsp oil

1 punnet cress, trimmed

SAVE EFFORT

Prepare to the end of step 3 up to
2 hours ahead. Cover the glaze
and chorizo oil and keep at room
temperature. Cover the melon and
chorizo and chill. Allow the chorizo
to come up to room temperature,
then complete the recipe to serve.

1 Halve the melon, then spoon out and discard the seeds. Cut each half into three wedges, then cut the skin off each wedge and chill until needed.

2 Put the balsamic vinegar and honey into a small pan and simmer gently for 5 minutes until syrupy. Leave to cool.

3 Cut the chorizo into small cubes. Heat the oil in a small frying pan and add the sausage cubes. Fry for 3 minutes until the chorizo is golden and has given up some of its oil. Strain into a small bowl and put the oil and chorizo to one side.

4 Put a melon wedge on each of six small plates, then sprinkle over some of the fried chorizo and cress. Finally, drizzle the chorizo oil and balsamic glaze over each plate. Serve immediately.

Camembert Melt

Hands-on time: 5 minutes
Cooking time: about 20 minutes

250g wooden-boxed (stapled not glued)
  Camembert

1½ tbsp white wine or cider (optional)

2 fresh thyme sprigs, leaves only

salt and ground black pepper

To serve

spears of steamed tenderstem broccoli

chunks of sourdough bread

rolls of ham

cornichons

1 Preheat the oven to 200°C (180°C fan oven) mark 6. Discard the lid of the Camembert box and any cloth wrapping. Take the cheese out of the box and unwrap, leaving it on the waxed paper. Slice off the top rind and discard. Return the cheese (on its paper), cut side up to the box and put on a baking sheet.

2 Season with salt and ground black pepper. Sprinkle over the alcohol, if you lik, and half the thyme. Cook in the oven for 15–20 minutes until the cheese is golden on top and melted inside. Transfer the box to a board, garnish with the remaining thyme and serve with a choice of dippers.

Serves 2

French Onion Soup

Hands-on time: 25 minutes
Cooking time: about 1 hour 10 minutes

2 tbsp olive oil

6 large onions, about 1.6kg (3½lb),
    finely sliced

2 tsp fresh thyme leaves, plus extra
    to garnish

500ml (17fl oz) cider

1 tsp caster sugar

1.4 litres (2½ pints) vegetable stock

6 small slices white bread

150g (5oz) Gruyère, grated

salt and freshly ground black pepper

1 Gently heat the oil in a large pan. Add the onions, thyme and a large pinch of salt. Cover and cook over a low heat for 30 minutes, stirring occasionally, until the onions are soft.

2 Pour over the cider and add the sugar. Turn up the heat and bubble, stirring frequently, until the cider has evaporated and the onions are well caramelised, about 30-40 minutes.

3 Add the stock and heat through. Check the seasoning. Preheat the grill to medium. Put the bread on a baking tray and lightly toast both sides under the grill. Divide the cheese equally among the toasts and grill until melted and bubbling.

4 To serve, divide the soup among six warmed soup bowls. Top each bowl with a cheese toast and garnish with a few thyme leaves and ground black pepper.

FREEZE AHEAD

Prepare to the end of step 2 up to two months ahead. Cool completely, then empty into a freezerproof bag and freeze. To serve, thaw completely and complete the recipe.

Serves 6

Pea, Parmesan and Chorizo Soup

Hands-on time: 15 minutes
Cooking time: about 10 minutes

1 tbsp olive oil

1 large onion, roughly chopped

40g (1½oz) Parmesan, grated

75g (3oz) chorizo, skinned and
    finely cubed

750g (1lb 11oz) frozen peas

1.2 litre (2¼ pints) hot vegetable stock

salt and freshly ground black pepper

1 Preheat the oven to 220°C (200°C fan oven) mark 7. In a large pan, heat the oil and fry the onion for 5 minutes.

2 Meanwhile, sprinkle the Parmesan over a small non-stick baking sheet and cook in the oven for 5 minutes until golden and bubbling. Then fry the chorizo in a small frying pan for 2–3 minutes until some of the oil has leaked out. Put to one side. Take the Parmesan out of oven, allow to harden slightly, then use a spatula to lift the cheese off the baking sheet. Put on to a wire rack to cool.

3 Add the peas and hot stock to the onion pan and bring to the boil. Take off the heat and blend until smooth. Put back into the pan and check the seasoning.

4 To serve, reheat the soup if necessary, then divide among six warmed soup bowls. Break the Parmesan into shards. Garnish the soups with Parmesan shards, chorizo and chorizo oil. Serve immediately.

SAVE EFFORT

Make to the end of step 3 up to 2 hours ahead. Chill the soup and store the Parmesan and chorizo (in its pan) at a cool room temperature. To serve, reheat the chorizo in pan and complete the recipe to serve.

Serves 6

Perfect Mussels

One of the most popular shellfish, mussels takes moments to cook.
Careful preparation is important, so give yourself enough time to
get the shellfish ready.

Cooking mussels

1. Scrape off the fibres attached to the shells (beards). If the mussels are very clean, give them a quick rinse under the cold tap. If they are very sandy, scrub them with a stiff brush.

2. If the shells have sizeable barnacles on them, it is best (though not essential) to remove them. Rap them sharply with a metal spoon or the back of a washing-up brush, then scrape off.

3. Discard any open mussels that don't shut when sharply tapped; this means they are dead and could be dangerous to eat.

1

4. In a large heavy-based pan, fry 2 finely chopped shallots and a generous handful of parsley in 25g (1oz) butter for about 2 minutes or until soft. Pour in 1cm (½in) dry white wine.

5. Add the mussels to the pan and cover tightly with a lid. Steam for 5–10 minutes until the shells open. Immediately take the pan away from the heat.

6. Using a slotted spoon, remove the mussels from the pan and discard any that haven't opened, then boil the cooking liquid rapidly to reduce. Pour over the mussels and serve immediately.

4

5

Moules Marinière

Hands-on time: 15 minutes
Cooking time: about 20 minutes

2kg (4½lb) fresh mussels, scrubbed,
  rinsed and beards removed (see
  Safety Tip, opposite)

25g (1oz) butter

4 shallots, finely chopped

2 garlic cloves, crushed

200ml (7fl oz) dry white wine

2 tbsp freshly chopped flat-leafed parsley

100ml (3½fl oz) single cream

salt and freshly ground black pepper

crusty bread to serve

1 Sort the mussels following the Safety
  Tip opposite. Clean under running
  water, removing any barnacles or
  stringy beards with a cutlery knife.

2 Heat the butter in a large non-stick
  lidded frying pan and sauté the
  shallots over a medium-high heat
  for about 10 minutes until soft.

3 Add the garlic, wine and half the
  parsley to the pan and bring to the
  boil. Tip in the mussels and reduce the

SAFETY TIP

- Mussels are sold either by weight
  or volume: 1.1 litres (2 pints) of
  mussels is roughly equivalent to
  900g (2lb).
- Do not buy mussels with cracked
  or open shells.
- To prepare fresh mussels, rinse
  them under cold running water
  to help rid them of any grit
  and sand. Using a small stiff
  brush, scrub the mussel shells

  thoroughly, to remove any grit
  and barnacles.
- Pull away the hairy 'beard',
  which protrudes from one side of
  the shell. Tap any open mussels
  sharply with the back of the
  knife or on the surface. If they
  refuse to close, throw them away.
  Rinse the mussels again under
  cold running water
  before cooking.

heat a little. Cover and cook for about 5 minutes until all the shells have opened; discard any mussels that remain closed.

4 Lift out the mussels with a slotted spoon and put into serving bowls, then cover with foil to keep warm.

Add the cream to the pan, season with salt and ground black pepper and cook for 1–2 minutes to heat through.

5 Pour a little sauce over the mussels and sprinkle with the rest of the parsley. Serve immediately with crusty bread.

Serves 4

Perfect Scallops and Oysters

Both of these delicately flavoured shellfish are contained within shells that can be a little tricky to open. Ask your fishmonger to prepare them if you prefer. The fish themselves have a marvellous taste..

Scallops can be eaten raw, either seasoned or marinated in citrus juice with seasonings. They take very little cooking, usually between 5 and 10 minutes.

Opening scallops

1. Hold the scallop with the flat half of the shell facing up. Firmly ease a very sharp small knife between the shells at a point close to the hinge.
2. Keeping the knife angled towards the flat shell, cut all along the shell surface until the two shells can be separated easily. Cut along the bottom of the rounded shell to release its contents. Cut loose the meat and the grey/orange coral and discard everything else.

3 Rinse off any grit, cut the coral
   from the round meat, and cut the
   little scrap of muscle from the edge
   of the meat

Oysters can be fried, poached
and grilled, or eaten straight from
the shell with red wine vinegar
flavoured with shallots, or just with
lemon juice.

Opening oysters

1 Hold the oyster in one hand with
   the flat half of the shell facing up,
   using a towel to protect your hand.
   Insert an oyster knife in the hinge
   and twist.
2 When the upper shell comes off,
   scrape off any shell and then cut
   under the oyster to release it from
   the shell.

Sizzling Scallops with Pancetta and Sage

Hands-on time: 15 minutes
Cooking time: about 15 minutes

1 tbsp sunflower oil

150g (5oz) pancetta cubes

6 fresh sage leaves, finely shredded

18 scallops (with or without the coral),
   cleaned

salt and freshly ground black pepper

balsamic glaze and 1 punnet cress
   to garnish

1 Heat ½ tbsp of the oil in a large frying
pan over a medium heat and fry the
pancetta for 8 minutes or until golden.
Add the sage leaves and fry for 1
minute more. Tip the mixture and any
oil into a bowl. Cover with foil.

SAVE EFFORT

You can fry the scallops as close
together as you like – it helps them
stay straight rather than tipping on
to their sides.

2 Pat the scallops dry with kitchen
paper and season well. Heat the
remaining oil in pancetta pan, turn up
the heat to high and fry the scallops
for about 4 minutes, turning halfway
during cooking time – they should
be lightly golden and feel springy
when pressed.

3 Divide the scallops and arrange
among six small plates, then spoon
pancetta mixture and any oil around
them. Dot with balsamic glaze and
scatter over cress. Serve immediately.

SAVE TIME

Fry pancetta up to a day ahead,
but do not add the sage. Tip into a
bowl, cover and chill. When ready
to serve, fry the pancetta for 2
minutes to reheat, add the sage and
complete the recipe.

George

Decadent Dinners

Vegetarian Pea Pithivier

Hands-on time: 30 minutes, plus chilling
Cooking time: about 55 minutes, plus cooling

175g (6oz) frozen peas

½ tbsp olive oil

2 onions, finely sliced

175g (6oz) full-fat cream cheese

a small handful of fresh parsley, finely chopped

½ tbsp wholegrain mustard

1 tbsp freshly chopped tarragon

40g (1½oz) fresh white breadcrumbs

plain flour to dust

500g pack puff pastry

1 medium egg, lightly beaten

salt and freshly ground black pepper

SAVE TIME

Prepare the pithivier to the end of step 3 up to one day ahead. To serve, reglaze with beaten egg and complete the recipe.

1 Take the peas out of the freezer and put to one side. Heat the oil in a medium pan and cook the onions for 10–15 minutes until softened. Empty into a large bowl and leave to cool.

2 Stir the cream cheese, parsley, mustard, tarragon, breadcrumbs, peas and plenty of seasoning into the cooled onion bowl.

3 Lightly flour a worksurface and roll out one-third of the pastry until it is 3mm (⅛in) thick. Cut out a 20.5cm (8in) pastry circle and put on a baking tray. Spoon the pea mixture on to the circle and, leaving a 3cm (1¼in) border of pastry around the edge, shape the filling into a flattened disc with straight edges, about 3cm (1¼in) tall. Brush the border around the filling with beaten egg. Next, roll out the remaining pastry as before, until it is 3mm (⅛in) thick. Place it over the filling, then smooth it down to get rid of any air bubbles. Press down firmly on the edges to seal, then trim into a

neat circle (using the base circle as a guide). Crimp the edges. Brush with beaten egg, then score the top lightly in a pattern like the spokes of a wheel. Chill for at least 1 hour.

4 Preheat the oven to 200°C (180°C fan oven) mark 6 and put a separate baking tray in the oven to heat up. Working quickly and carefully, transfer the prepared pithivier on to the hot baking tray and cook in the oven for 30-40 minutes until deep golden. Serve warm or at room temperature.

Serves 6

Tomato Tarte Tatin

Hands-on time: 25 minutes
Cooking time: about 1 hour 10 minutes

½ tbsp olive oil

3 red onions, finely sliced

2 fresh thyme sprigs, leaves only, plus
  extra to garnish

50g (2oz) caster sugar

a small knob of butter

½ tbsp balsamic vinegar

650g (1lb 7oz) plum tomatoes, halved

375g pack ready-rolled puff pastry

green salad to serve

1 Heat the oil in a large pan, add the
   onions, cover and cook gently for
   15 minutes. Take off the lid, turn
   up the heat and cook, stirring, for 5
   minutes or until the onions begin to
   caramelise. Stir in the thyme leaves
   and put to one side.

2 Preheat the oven to 220°C (200°C
   fan oven) mark 7. Put a heavy-based
   24cm (9½in) round casserole dish
   or ovenproof frying pan over a low
   heat. Add the sugar and 50ml (2fl
   oz) water and heat gently, stirring,
   until the sugar dissolves, then turn

up the heat and allow the sugar to
caramelise (do not stir, just swirl the
pan occasionally). When the sugar is
deeply caramelised (it should be the
colour of honey), carefully add the
butter and vinegar – it will spit and
hiss. Stir to combine, then take the
pan off the heat.

3 Arrange the tomatoes, cut side down,
   in a single layer in the bottom of
   the casserole or pan. Cover with the
   cooked onions. Unroll the pastry
   and cut out a circle 1cm (½in) larger
   than the base of the casserole or pan
   (it's fine to use trimmings to make a
   complete circle). Position the pastry
   on top of the onions and then tuck in
   the edges.

4 Cook in the oven for 30–40 minutes
   until the pastry is deep golden. Take
   out of the oven and leave to rest for 5
   minutes. Invert on to a plate, garnish
   with thyme leaves and serve with a
   green salad.

Serves 4

Oriental Baked Tofu

Hands-on time: 10 minutes
Cooking time: 15 minutes

150g (5oz) regular tofu

½ a thinly sliced garlic clove

2cm (¾in) fresh root ginger,
   cut into matchsticks

1 tsp soy sauce

freshly ground black pepper

a small handful of fresh coriander

a few chilli rings

lime wedges to serve

SAVE EFFORT

Assemble the parcel and put on
a tray up to 3 hours ahead. Chill.
Complete the recipe to serve.

1 Preheat the oven to 220°C (200°C fan oven) mark 7. Stack two 30.5cm (12in) sheets of greaseproof paper, baking parchment or foil on top of each other and put the tofu on one side.

2 Sprinkle over the garlic slices, ginger, soy sauce and some ground black pepper. Fold paper/parchment/foil over, then fold in the edges to seal. Put parcel on a baking sheet and cook for 15 minutes. Open and sprinkle over a small handful of fresh coriander and a few chilli rings. Serve with lime wedges.

Serves 1

Broccoli, Gorgonzola and Walnut Quiche

Hands-on time: 10 minutes, plus chilling
Cooking time: about 1 hour

400g (14oz) shortcrust pastry
plain flour to dust
150g (5oz) broccoli florets
100g (3½oz) crumbled Gorgonzola
2 medium eggs
1 egg yolk
300ml (½ pint) double cream
25g (1oz) roughly chopped walnut halves
salt and freshly ground black pepper

1 Preheat the oven to 200°C (180°C fan oven) mark 6. Roll out the pastry on a floured worksurface until it is the thickness of a £1 coin, then use to line a 23 × 2.5cm (9 × 1in) deep fluted tart tin. Prick the base all over and chill for 15 minutes. Blind bake for 20 minutes, removing the beans and paper for the last 5 minutes of the cooking. Lower the oven setting to 150°C (130°C fan oven) mark 2.

2 Cook the broccoli florets in boiling water for 3 minutes, then drain and dry on kitchen paper. Arrange the broccoli in the pastry case. Dot with Gorgonzola. Whisk together the eggs, egg yolk, cream and some seasoning, then pour into the case. Scatter over the walnuts and cook the quiche for 40 minutes or until the filling is set. Serve warm or at room temperature.

FREEZE AHEAD

Complete the quiche up to one month in advance. Cool in the tin, then wrap in clingfilm and freeze. To serve, thaw completely, then serve at room temperature or gently reheat for 20 minutes in a preheated 150°C (130°C fan oven) mark 2 oven.

Serves 6

Deluxe Fig and Ham Salad

Hands-on time: 15 minutes
cooking time: about 5 minutes

200g (7oz) fine green beans, ends trimmed

3 tbsp extra virgin olive oil

4 slices white sourdough bread, cut into large cubes

4 Little Gem lettuces, quartered lengthways

85g pack Parma ham

4 figs, quartered

1 tsp Dijon mustard

½ tbsp cider or white wine vinegar

alt and freshly ground black pepper

1 Bring a small pan of water to the boil and cook the beans for 4 minutes or until tender. Drain and leave in a colander to steam dry until needed.

2 Heat 1 tbsp of the oil in a large frying pan and fry the bread cubes, tossing frequently, until golden and crisp. Season with salt and leave to cool.

3 Arrange the lettuce quarters cut side up on a large platter. Roughly rip the Parma ham slices in half lengthways and weave among the lettuce quarters. Dot over the figs, beans and toasted bread cubes.

4 In a small jug, mix together the Dijon mustard, vinegar, remaining oil and some seasoning. Drizzle over the salad and serve.

SAVE EFFORT

This decadent salad is perfect for a dinner party. If you're not a fan of figs, use peeled, stoned and sliced fresh peaches instead.

Lobster Thermidor

🍴 **Hands-on time:** 20 minutes
Cooking time: about 10 minutes

700g (1½lb) cooked whole lobster

150ml (¼ pint) double cream

1 tsp English mustard

40g (1½oz) butter

finely grated zest of ½ lemon

40g (1½oz) Parmesan, grated

1 tbsp chopped fresh chives,
  plus extra to garnish

salt and ground black pepper

potato wedges and green salad to serve

1 Twist the claws off the lobster. Hit the heavy side of a claw sharply with the heel of a large knife, to embed the knife (keeping fingers well away). Now twist the knife until the claw cracks open. Pick the meat from the claw, taking care not to include the bone-like tendon, then roughly chop and put into a bowl. Repeat with the remaining claw.

2 Next twist off the legs (they should be attached to a feathery gill, which you should discard). If you have time, crack the shell of the legs with a knife and ease out the meat with a toothpick – add the meat to the bowl. Now fully extend the lobster body in front of you (back facing up), lay on a board and push the tip of a large knife into the lobster just below the head. Now cut down the length of the back to halve the lobster. Ease out the white meat, roughly chop and add to the bowl. Wash the halved shells and set on a baking tray.

3 Preheat the oven to 200°C (180°C fan oven) mark 6. Put the cream, mustard, butter and lemon zest into a medium pan. Heat gently, stirring, and simmer for 3–5 minutes or until the mixture is the consistency of Greek yogurt. Stir in the lobster meat, Parmesan and most of the chives, then check the seasoning. Spoon the mixture back into the shells.

4 Cook for 5 minutes or until lightly golden and bubbling. Garnish with chives and serve with Thyme Chunky Potato Wedges and a green salad.

An expensive treat, but well worth the cost. If you don't fancy halving and picking the lobster, or have no time to, then ask your fishmonger to do the hard work for you.

Serves 2

Oriental Baked Fish

Hands-on time: 10 minutes
Cooking time: about 20 minutes

1.1kg (2½lb) cod fillets

1 garlic clove, thinly sliced

3cm (1½in) piece fresh root ginger, cut into matchsticks

1 tbsp fish sauce

freshly ground black pepper

a large handful of fresh coriander to garnish

1 red chilli, sliced into rings to garnish (see Safety Tip, page 26)

lime wedges to serve

SAVE TIME

If you can't find larger fillets, use ready-portioned smaller ones. Salmon also works well.

SAVE EFFORT

Assemble the parcel and put on a tray up to 3 hours ahead. Chill. Complete the recipe to serve.

1 Preheat the oven to 220°C (200°C fan oven) mark 7. Stack two large sheets of greaseproof paper, baking parchment or foil (a little longer than your fish fillets) on top of each other on a worksurface. Put the fish fillets side by side (overlapping a little) on to one side of the paper. Sprinkle over the garlic and ginger, then pour the fish sauce down the length of the fish. Season with ground black pepper. Fold the empty side of the paper/ parchment/foil over to cover the fish, then fold each edge in a few times to seal the parcel.

2 Transfer the parcel to a large, lipped baking tray and roast for 15–20 minutes or until the fish feels firm when pressed through the parcel.

3 Slide the unopened parcel on to a large board and open it at the table. Scatter over the coriander and chilli and serve with lime wedges.

Wrapped Monkfish with Milanese Risotto

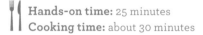

Hands-on time: 25 minutes
Cooking time: about 30 minutes

6 × 175g (6oz) monkfish fillets, skinless

6 Parma ham slices

25g (1oz) butter

salt and freshly ground black pepper

For the risotto

1 tbsp extra virgin olive oil,
    plus extra to drizzle

1 onion, finely chopped

2 large pinches of saffron

300g (11oz) risotto rice

125ml (4fl oz) dry white wine

1.4 litre (2½ pint) fish or vegetable stock

200g (7oz) fine asparagus,
    cut into 2.5cm (1in) pieces

200g (7oz) peas, fresh or frozen

1 large courgette, cut into
    1cm (½in) pieces

75g (3oz) Parmesan, grated,
    plus shavings to serve

large handful pea shoots

1 Start by making the risotto. Heat the oil in a large pan and fry the onion for 10 minutes until softened. Meanwhile, wrap each fish fillet in a slice of Parma ham, season and put to one side.

2 Stir the saffron and rice into onion pan. Cook, stirring, for 1 minute, then add the wine and leave to bubble for a few minutes. Add a quarter of the stock and cook, stirring occasionally, until most of it has been absorbed. Continue adding big glugs of stock, stirring occasionally, until the rice is nearly tender, about 18 minutes (you may not need all the stock).

3 A few minutes before the rice is ready, add the asparagus, peas and courgette. When the rice is cooked and the veg are tender, take off the heat and stir in the Parmesan. Check the seasoning.

4 10 minutes before the rice is due to be ready, heat the butter in a large frying pan over a medium heat until foaming. Cook the monkfish parcels for 10 minutes, turning once, until cooked through.

SAVE TIME

Prepare to the end of step 2 up to a day ahead. Spread the risotto on a tray. When cool, cover and chill. Cover and chill the wrapped fish. To serve, put the risotto into a pan, add some stock and reheat (stirring). Complete the recipe to serve.

Serves 6

Couscous-crusted Lamb

Hands-on time: 15 minutes
Cooking time: about 20 minutes

75g (3oz) couscous

3 racks of lamb, excess fat trimmed off

25g (1oz) each dried cranberries and
    pistachios, finely chopped

2 medium eggs

1½ tsp wholegrain mustard

1½ tsp dried mint

salt and freshly ground black pepper

1 Put the couscous into a bowl and
pour over 125ml (4fl oz) boiling water.
Cover with clingfilm and put to one
side for 10 minutes.

2 Meanwhile, trim any membrane from
the lamb racks, scrape the bones clean
using a small knife and pat the meat
dry. Put the lamb racks on to a large
baking tray.

3 Preheat the oven to 200°C (180°C fan
oven) mark 6. Use a fork to fluff up the
couscous, then stir in the cranberries,
pistachios, eggs, mustard, mint and
some seasoning. Press a third of the
couscous crust on top of the meat on
each lamb rack.

4 Cook the lamb for 15-20 minutes for
pink meat, or longer if you prefer.
Transfer the racks to a board, cover
with foil and leave to rest for 5 minutes
before carving and serving.

FREEZE AHEAD

Prepare to the end of step 3 up to
one month ahead. Wrap the baking
tray well in clingfilm, then freeze. To
serve, thaw overnight in the fridge,
unwrap and complete the recipe.

Serves 6

Roast Lamb and Boulangère Potatoes

Hands-on time: 25 minutes
Cooking time: about 1½ hours, plus resting

2kg (4½lb) Maris Piper potatoes, thinly sliced into rounds – a mandolin is ideal for this

1 large onion, thinly sliced

10 thyme sprigs

400ml (14fl oz) hot chicken stock

2 camomile teabags

2 tsp sunflower oil

1.6kg (3½lb) lamb shoulder at room temperature

salt and freshly ground black pepper

mint sauce or redcurrant jelly and seasonal vegetables to serve

1 Preheat the oven to 200°C (180°C fan oven) mark 6. Layer the potato slices, onion and half the thyme in a 2.5 litre (4¼ pint) heatproof serving dish, seasoning as you go. Pour the hot stock over. Put a large wire rack over the dish.

2 Empty the contents of the camomile teabags into a small bowl (discard the bags). Stir in the leaves from the remaining thyme, some seasoning and the oil. Rub the camomile mixture over the lamb. Sit the lamb on the wire rack on top of the dish. Cover everything with foil.

3 Carefully transfer the dish to the oven and roast for 1 hour. Uncover and cook for 30 minutes more (the lamb should be cooked to medium) or until the lamb is cooked to your liking and the potatoes are tender and golden.

4 Transfer the lamb to a board, cover with foil and leave to rest for 20 minutes; keep the potatoes warm in the oven. Serve the lamb and potatoes with mint sauce or redcurrant jelly and seasonal vegetables.

Serves 8

Rich Beef Casserole

Hands-on time: 25 minutes
Cooking time: about 2½ hours

1.2kg (2lb 11oz) braising steak, cut into
    4cm (1½in) cubes

2 tbsp vegetable oil

8 shallots, halved

250g (9oz) Portabella mushrooms,
    thickly sliced

1 tbsp plain flour

150ml (5fl oz) red wine

800ml (1 pint 7fl oz) beef stock

a handful of dried wild mushrooms

3 fresh thyme sprigs

1 bay leaf

25g (1oz) cornflour

a handful of fresh parsley, chopped

salt and freshly ground black pepper

1 Preheat the oven to 160°C (140°C fan
   oven) mark 3. Pat the beef dry with
   kitchen paper and season. Heat 1½
   tbsp of the oil in a large ovenproof
   casserole dish and brown beef in
   batches. Put to one side.

2 Heat the remaining oil and fry the
   shallots for 2–3 minutes until golden,
   then add the Portabella mushrooms
   and fry for 2–3 minutes until softened.

3 Put the beef back into the pan with
   any juices and stir in the flour. Add the
   wine, stock, dried mushrooms, thyme
   and bay leaf. Bring to the boil, then
   cover and cook in the oven for 2 hours
   or until the beef is tender.

4 Strain the stew, put the beef mixture
   to one side and pour the liquid back
   into the pan. In a small bowl, mix
   together the cornflour and 3 tbsp
   water. Add to the pan and heat on the
   hob. Boil the sauce for 4–5 minutes,
   stirring constantly until the mixture
   thickens. Add the strained beef
   mixture and heat through (don't boil
   or the meat will toughen). Remove
   the thyme sprigs and bay leaf and
   discard. Add the parsley and check
   the seasoning. Serve immediately.

Serves 6

Pork and Sage Parcel

Hands-on time: 15 minutes
Cooking time: about 30 minutes

375g pack ready-rolled puff pastry

1 medium egg, beaten

75g (3oz) pancetta slices

2 × 400g (14oz) pork fillets,
    membrane removed

1 tbsp freshly chopped sage

freshly ground black pepper

Roast Baby Potatoes (see page 78),
    Spiced Red Cabbage (see page 80),
    Thyme Tomatoes (see page 82) and
    apple sauce to serve

1 Preheat the oven to 220°C (200°C fan
   oven) mark 7. Unroll the puff pastry
   and cut out a 11.5 × 28cm (4½ × 11in)
   rectangle. Transfer to a baking tray
   and brush with some of the egg.

2 Arrange the pancetta slices side by
   side on a board, overlapping them
   a little. Lay one of the pork fillets
   horizontally across the middle of the
   pancetta slices. Press the sage on top
   of the pork, then season well with
   ground black pepper. Top with the
   second pork fillet.

3 Fold the pancetta around the pork
   and put the wrapped fillet, seam-
   side down, on top of the pastry base.
   Cut 5mm (¼in) wide strips from the
   remaining pastry, each long enough
   to cover the fillet. Arrange the pastry
   strips in a criss-cross pattern over the
   pork, pressing the ends of the strips to
   the base to help them stick. Brush the
   strips with the rest of the beaten egg.

4 Cook the pork parcel for 25–30
   minutes until the pastry is dark
   golden. Transfer to a board, cover with
   foil and leave to rest for 10 minutes.
   Serve in slices with Roast Baby
   Potatoes, Spiced Red Cabbage, Thyme
   Tomatoes and some apple sauce.

SAVE EFFORT

Make to the end of step 3 up to
3 hours ahead. Chill. Complete the
recipe to serve, cooking the parcel
for 30–35 minutes.

Serves 6

Roast Rolled Sirloin of Beef with Port Gravy

Hands-on time: 20 minutes, plus marinating
Cooking time: about 1½ hours (depends on meat thickness)

1.5-2kg (3¼-4½lb) rolled beef
    sirloin joint

4 fresh rosemary sprigs, leaves removed
    and finely chopped

2 garlic cloves, finely chopped

2 tbsp olive oil

salt and freshly ground black pepper

For the gravy

2 tbsp plain flour

400ml (14fl oz) beef stock

100ml (3½fl oz) port

1 tbsp redcurrant jelly

SAVE EFFORT

Prepare to the end of step 1 up to a day ahead. Cover and chill. Allow to reach room temperature, then complete the recipe.

1 Weigh the beef; calculate the cooking time: allow 5–15 minutes per 450g (1lb) depending on how well you like it cooked (rare to well done). Put the joint into a roasting tin that just holds it. Mix the rosemary, garlic, oil and lots of seasoning. Rub the mixture over the joint, then cover with clingfilm and leave for 1-3 hours.

2 When the beef has marinated, preheat the oven to 200°C (180°C fan oven) mark 6. Roast the beef for 20 minutes, then lower the oven setting to 180°C (160°C fan oven) mark 4 and cook for your calculated time.

3 When the beef is cooked to your liking, transfer to a board, cover with foil and rest for 30 minutes.

4 To make the gravy, spoon out most of the fat from the beef tin. Put the tin over a medium heat; stir in the flour. Cook for 1 minute, mixing well, then gradually mix in the stock. Bubble for

3 minutes, stirring occasionally, then pour in the port. Scrape the base of the tin to release the sticky bits, and simmer for 5 minutes. Stir in the jelly until dissolved, then strain through a sieve into a pan. Check seasoning.

5 Reheat the gravy and serve with the roast beef.

Serves 6–8

Perfect Roast Pork Belly

🍴 **Hands-on time:** 15 minutes, plus drying and resting
Cooking time: about 3½ hours

1.5kg (3¼lb) piece pork belly
roast potatoes, kale and apple sauce
  to serve

1 Using a small sharp knife, score lines into the skin (cutting into the fat) about 1cm (½in) apart, but not so deep that you cut into the meat. Pat the pork completely dry, then leave uncovered at room temperature to air dry for about 45 minutes.

2 Preheat the oven to 220°C (200°C fan oven) mark 7. Rub lots of salt over the pork skin. Rest a wire rack above a deep roasting tin and put the pork skin-side up on the rack. Roast for 30 minutes, then lower the oven setting to 170°C (150°C fan oven) mark 3 and continue cooking for 3 hours – by this stage the crackling should be crisp and golden (if not, don't panic – see Save Effort, right).

3 Transfer the pork to a board and use a sharp knife to slice off the crackling in one piece (about the outer 2cm/¾in). Cover the pork meat loosely with foil and leave to rest for 30–40 minutes.

4 Cut the crackling into six long strips, then cut the pork belly into six neat squares. Serve each square topped with a strip of crackling together with roast potatoes, kale and apple sauce.

SAVE EFFORT

If your crackling isn't as crispy as you'd like, you can still rescue it. Remove the crackling and preheat the grill to medium-high. Put the whole piece of crackling on a baking tray and grill until crisp and puffed (watch carefully to avoid scorching, turning the tray to avoid any hot spots). Complete the recipe to serve.

Serves 6

Five-spice Duck with Port Plums

Hands-on time: 20 minutes
Cooking time: about 40 minutes

4 large duck breasts, each about
   225g (8oz)

1 tbsp Chinese five-spice powder

3 shallots, finely sliced

1 star anise (optional)

4 large plums, halved and stoned

200ml (7fl oz) ruby port

150ml (5fl oz) beef stock

1 Preheat the oven to 200°C (180°C fan oven) mark 6. Score the skin of each duck breast into a diamond pattern, taking care not to cut through into the meat. Rub ¼ tbsp of the spice over the skin of each breast.

2 Gently heat a large frying pan over a low heat. Add the duck breasts, skin side down, and leave to cook for 10–15 minutes (without turning) until some of the fat has rendered out and the skin is crisp and golden (the actual meat should not have started cooking, just the skin and fat). Pour off the excess fat into a bowl. Arrange the breasts skin side up on a baking tray in a single layer.

3 Roast the duck breasts on the baking tray in the oven for 14–16 minutes for pink meat (cook for shorter or longer as you prefer). Meanwhile, heat 1 tbsp of the reserved duck fat in the empty frying pan and cook the shallots and star anise, if you like, for 3–5 minutes. Add the plum halves, cut side down, and fry for a few minutes.

4 When the duck is cooked to your liking, transfer the breasts to a board. Cover with foil and lay over a clean teatowel to keep in the heat. Leave to rest for 10 minutes.

5 Add the port to the plum pan, turn up the heat and bubble until most of the liquid has evaporated. Add the stock and simmer for a few minutes until it turns syrupy.

6 Thickly slice the breasts and serve with the plums and sauce.

Prepare the duck breasts to the end of step 2 up to an hour ahead. Prepare the plums and sauce to the end of step 6. Put to one side. To serve, roast the duck and gently reheat the plum sauce (you may need to add a touch more stock).

Chill any leftover duck fat and use it to roast vegetables or potatoes for another meal. The fat will keep in the fridge for up to a week.

Serves 4

Perfect Cheese

Probably the best place to buy cheese is from a specialist cheese shop if you are lucky enough to have access to one, otherwise many supermarkets have a fresh cheese counter offering a good variety of farmhouse and factory-made cheeses.

Buying and storing cheese

Probably the best place to buy cheese is from a specialist cheese shop if you are lucky enough to have access to one, otherwise many supermarkets have a fresh cheese counter offering a good variety of farmhouse and factory-made cheeses.

Try to taste first before you commit to buying a cheese, as artisan cheeses will vary within, as well as across, varieties – some cheeses differ according to the time of year, and certain varieties are seasonal. Once you have made your choice, make sure the cheese is freshly sliced to your requirements. Buy only as much or as little as you think you need – central heating and refrigeration will dry out the cheese once you get it home.

The best way to store cheese is to wrap it in waxed paper then to put into an unsealed plastic food bag or cheese box. Keep in the fridge in the least cold area away from the freezer compartment. If you have a whole, rinded cheese, cover the cut surface with clingfilm.

To enjoy cheese at its best, you should always remove it from the fridge at least 2 hours before serving to bring it to room temperature. Loosen the wrapping and remove it just before serving. Provide at least two knives for cutting, so that there is a separate one for blue cheese.

Buying cheese for vegetarians

Some vegetarians prefer to avoid cheeses that have been produced by the traditional method, because this uses animal-derived rennet; however, most supermarkets and cheese shops now stock an excellent range of vegetarian cheeses, produced using vegetarian rennet. Always check the label when buying.

Selecting for a cheeseboard

Choosing cheeses for a cheeseboard is a matter of satisfying everyone's taste, so a range of flavours from mild to strong, and a variety of textures, is important. Think about shapes and colours, too. If you are serving four cheeses, choose one hard, one soft, one blue and one goat's cheese. If you are buying from a specialist cheese shop or a supermarket cheese counter, ask to try a piece first so that you know what you are getting and can balance the flavours. It is a question of quality rather than quantity, as a few excellent cheeses are more appealing than five or six with competing flavours.

To accompany your cheeses, choose crisp apples, juicy pears, grapes or figs. Very mild, soft goat's cheeses can be eaten with strawberries; slightly harder ones go well with cherry tomatoes or olives. Salad leaves should be bitter – try some chicory, frisée or rocket. Walnuts and celery are excellent with blue cheese. Oatcakes, wheat wafers and digestive biscuits go well with most cheeses, and if you want to serve bread, make sure it is fresh and crusty. Butter should be unsalted.

As for when you serve cheese, rounding off the meal with the cheeseboard is the norm in this country, but the French custom of moving from main course to cheese course is worth considering. It enables you to savour the cheeses before you are too full to enjoy them, and you can carry on drinking the same wine.

Desserts and Drinks

Drinks Guide

For large gatherings, offer one white and one red wine, sticking to around 12.5% alcohol, and have plenty of different soft drinks. Provide beer and lager if you like, but avoid spirits. Wines, sparkling wines and hot or cold punches are ideal party drinks.

For very large numbers, buy wines and champagne on a sale-or-return basis from a wine merchant. Mineral water, fruit juices and soft drinks can also be bought in this way. Most supermarkets will also allow this, provided the returned bottles are undamaged – check first.

Wine boxes are good value and it is worth asking your local wine merchant for their advice – some are better than others. If you prefer to serve wine from the bottle, look at the cost-saving potential of buying by the case.

When it comes to choosing wine it makes sense to find a supplier you can trust, whether it be a supermarket, wine merchant or warehouse. If you opt for something different, just buy one bottle and see if you enjoy it.

Generally, red wine goes best with red meats, and white wine is the better complement to fish, chicken and light meats, but there really are no longer any hard-and-fast rules.

For an aperitif, it is nice to serve a glass of chilled champagne or sparkling wine, or perhaps dry sherry.

Avoid sweet drinks, or spirits with a high alcohol content, as these tend to take the edge off the appetite, rather than stimulating it. Wine or sherry can be served with a soup course. A full-bodied red wine is an excellent accompaniment to the cheeseboard, although some people prefer to drink port with their cheese. You may wish to serve a dessert wine, such as Sauternes, or a glass of fruity demi-sec champagne. Coffee follows, with brandy and liqueurs if you like.

How much to buy?

If you allow one 75cl bottle of wine per head you should have more than enough. One standard 75cl bottle of wine, champagne or sparkling wine will give six glasses. A litre bottle will provide eight glasses. For a dinner party, allow one or two glasses of wine as an aperitif, one or two glasses with the first course, two glasses with the main course and another with the dessert or cheese.

Remember to buy plenty of mineral water – sparkling and still – and fresh fruit juices. For every ten guests, buy two 1.5 litre bottles of sparkling water and three similar-sized bottles of still water.

Serving wine

Warm white wine and champagne is inexcusable, and chilled red wine (unless young and intended for serving cold) is not pleasant. The ideal temperature for red wine is 15–18°C, with the more tannic wines benefiting from the higher temperature. For whites, the more powerful wines, like Chardonnay, should be served cool rather than cold, at 11–15°C, while other whites should be properly cold, at around 6–10°C. Party food will probably take up your fridge space, so you will need plenty of ice to keep drinks cool.

If you have a lot of wine to chill, use the bath. About an hour before the party, half-fill the bath with ice, pour in some cold water and stand the bottles upright, making sure the ice and water come up to their necks. Alternatively, use a clean plastic dustbin or cool boxes as containers. (Some hire companies will loan plastic bins for cooling wines.)

A large block of ice added to chilled water is a good idea. Make this by filling a large strong plastic bag with water, seal securely and place in the freezer until frozen.

Wine and party drink checklist:

- ❑ Champagne and sparkling wine
- ❑ Red wine
- ❑ White wine
- ❑ Beer and lager
- ❑ Mineral water, sparkling and natural
- ❑ Real fruit juices
- ❑ Other soft drinks and squashes
- ❑ Dessert wine or sweet sparkling wine
- ❑ Low-alcohol/alcohol-free wines, beer and lager
- ❑ Liqueurs, brandies etc., for cocktails
- ❑ Mixers
- ❑ Fail-safe corkscrews and wine-bottle stoppers – to 're-cork' opened wine bottles
- ❑ Plenty of ice and reusable ice packs.

Quantity Guide: drinks to the bottle
(using a standard size 100ml (3½fl oz) wine glass)

Sherry, port, vermouth	12 glasses
Single measure of spirits	30
'Split' – 200ml (7fl oz) soda, tonic, ginger ale	2–3
Table wine (75cl)	6
Table wine (1 litre)	8
Fruit juices – 600ml (1 pint)	4–6
Fruit cordial – 1 litre (1¾ pints) bottle diluted with 4 litres (7 pints) water	20–26
Punch – 1.7 litres (3 pints)	6–8

Cheat's Tiramisu

🍴 **Hands-on time:** 15 minutes

375g (13oz) mascarpone

75g (3oz) plain chocolate, finely chopped

2 medium eggs

75g (3oz) caster sugar

175–200g (6–7oz) chocolate loaf cake or brownies, roughly chopped

6 tbsp Tia Maria liqueur

cocoa powder to dust

gold leaf to sprinkle

1 Mix the mascarpone and chocolate together in a large bowl until combined. In a separate medium bowl, beat together the eggs and sugar using a hand-held electric whisk for about 5 minutes until pale and moussey. Use a large metal spoon to fold the egg mixture into the mascarpone bowl.

2 Divide half the chocolate loaf cake or brownies among six large glasses, then drizzle ½ tbsp of liqueur into each glass. Next, divide half the mascarpone mixture equally among the glasses. Repeat the layering process once more.

3 Cut a star template from a sheet of paper. Lay over one glass and dust with cocoa powder. Repeat with the remaining glasses and sprinkle gold leaf over each pudding. Serve immediately.

Note: As this pudding contains raw eggs, buy those with the British Lion mark and don't serve to vulnerable groups.

Serves 6

Perfect Coulis and Custards

Perfect as an accompaniment to many desserts, a simple vanilla custard can be served hot or cold. Chilled fruit purées are great with ice cream and meringues.

Vanilla Custard

To serve eight, you will need: 600ml (1 pint) full-fat milk, 1 vanilla pod or 1 tbsp vanilla extract, 6 large egg yolks, 2 tbsp golden caster sugar, 2 tbsp cornflour.

SAVE TIME

Make the custard up to 4 hours in advance. If you are not serving the custard immediately, pour it into a jug. Cover the surface with a round of wet greaseproof paper to prevent a skin from forming, then cover with clingfilm and chill. To serve hot, reheat very gently.

1 Pour the milk into a pan. Split the vanilla pod and scrape the seeds into the pan, then drop in the pod. Or pour in the vanilla extract. Bring to the boil, then turn off the heat and leave to cool for 5 minutes.

2 Put the egg yolks, sugar and cornflour into a bowl and whisk to blend. Remove the vanilla pod from the milk and gradually whisk the warm milk into the egg mixture.

3 Rinse out the pan. Pour the custard back into the pan and heat gently, stirring constantly, for 2–3 minutes. The mixture should be thick enough to coat the back of a wooden spoon in a thin layer. Take the pan off the heat.

Raspberry Coulis

To serve four to six, you will need:
225g (8oz) raspberries, 2 tbsp Kirsch
or framboise eau de vie (optional),
icing sugar to taste.

1 Put the raspberries into a blender
   or food processor with the Kirsch
   or eau de vie, if you like. Whiz
   until they are completely puréed.
2 Transfer the purée to a fine sieve
   and press and scrape it through
   the sieve until nothing is left
   but the dry pips.
3 Sweeten with icing sugar to taste
   and chill until needed.

SAVE EFFORT

For an easy way to make a new
sauce, use different soft fruits and
liqueurs. For example, try crème
de cassis with blackcurrants or
Amaretto with apricots.

1

2

Hazelnut and Raspberry Meringue Cake

🍴 **Hands-on time:** 25 minutes
Cooking time: about 40 minutes, plus cooling

5 medium egg whites

275g (10oz) caster sugar

75g (3oz) hazelnuts, roasted and finely chopped

300ml (½ pint) double cream

2 tbsp icing sugar, sifted

75–100 g (3–3½oz) frozen raspberries, thawed

40g (1½oz) plain chocolate, melted

1 Preheat the oven to 160°C (140°C fan oven) mark 3. Line two baking sheets with parchment and draw a 20.5cm (8in) circle on each sheet. Flip the baking parchment over so the ink is on the bottom.

2 Whisk the egg whites in a large bowl until stiff but not dry. Gradually add the caster sugar, mixing well after each addition, until thick and glossy. Quickly beat in the hazelnuts.

3 Divide the meringue mixture equally between the prepared baking sheets and smooth into a circle inside the marked lines. Bake for 30–40 minutes until lightly golden and easy to peel away from the paper. Leave to cool completely on the baking sheet – they may crack slightly.

4 Pour the cream into a bowl. Add the icing sugar and whip until the mixture just holds its shape. Tip in the raspberries and lightly whisk to break up the fruit.

5 Put one of the meringue discs on a serving plate. Cover with the raspberry cream and top with the remaining meringue disc. Use a teaspoon to drizzle over the melted chocolate and serve.

FREEZE AHEAD
Prepare to the end of step 3 up to one month ahead. Put both meringues on one baking sheet. Wrap in clingfilm and freeze. To serve, thaw and complete the recipe.

Serves 8

Chocolate Orange Cheesecake

Hands-on time: 20 minutes, plus chilling
Cooking time: about 40 minutes, plus cooling

For the base

50g (2oz) butter, melted, plus extra to grease

200g (7oz) dark chocolate digestives, finely crushed

For the filling

500g (1lb 2oz) cream cheese

150ml (5fl oz) soured cream

200g (7oz) caster sugar

1½ tbsp plain flour

1 tsp vanilla extract

grated zest of 1 orange

2 medium eggs, separated

To decorate

150g (5oz) plain chocolate, chopped

1 Grease a 20.5cm (8in) springform tin. Mix the butter and crushed biscuits together and press into the base. Chill for 15 minutes.

2 Preheat the oven to 180°C (160°C fan oven) mark 4. In a large bowl, whisk together all the filling ingredients, except the egg whites, until smooth. Whisk the egg whites in a separate bowl until soft peak stage. Use a large metal spoon to mix a spoonful of the whites into the cream cheese mixture, then fold in the remaining whites.

3 Pour the mixture into the tin and level. Bake for 35–40 minutes until lightly golden – the filling will firm up on chilling. Cool, it may crack on top, but this will be covered by the decoration. Chill for 2 hours or overnight.

4 Melt the chocolate in a heatproof bowl over a pan of gently simmering water (make sure the base of the bowl doesn't touch the water), then pour on to a baking sheet. Chill for 10 minutes until just set but not solid. Pull a large knife towards you across the chocolate to make a curl. Repeat until you've made enough curls to cover the cheesecake. Take the cheesecake out of the tin and put on a serving plate. Scatter over the chocolate curls and serve in slices.

Serves 8

Chocolate Torte

Hands-on time: 15 minutes, plus chilling
Cooking time: 5 minutes

200g (7oz) plain chocolate, broken
    into pieces

25g (1oz) butter, melted, plus extra
    to grease

1½ tbsp golden syrup

125g (4oz) butter biscuits, finely crushed

40g (1½oz) icing sugar

300ml (½ pint) double cream,
    at room temperature

2–3 tbsp Amaretto (optional)

crème fraîche to serve

To decorate

plain chocolate, grated

raspberries

icing sugar to dust

SAVE TIME

Make to end of step 3 up to a day
ahead. Complete the recipe to serve.

1 Melt the chocolate in a heatproof bowl
set over a pan of gently simmering
water. Leave to cool for 10 minutes.
Grease and line the sides of a 20.5cm
(8in) loose-bottomed cake tin with
greaseproof paper.

2 In a medium bowl, mix together
butter, golden syrup and crushed
biscuits. Press the mixture into the
base of the prepared tin.

3 Sift the icing sugar into a separate
bowl. Pour in the cream and Amaretto,
if you like, and whip until the cream
just holds its shape. Using a metal
spoon, fold the cooled chocolate into
the cream mix. Spoon the chocolate
mixture into the prepared cake tin,
level the surface, cover and chill until
ready to serve.

4 Transfer the torte to a serving plate.
Peel off the lining paper and scatter
over some grated plain chocolate. Dot
over a few raspberries and lightly dust
with icing sugar. Serve in slices with
crème fraîche.

Serves 10

Molten Chocolate Parcels

Hands-on time: 25 minutes, plus chilling
Cooking time: about 20 minutes, plus cooling

250g (9oz) dark chocolate, chopped

60g (2½oz) butter, at room temperature

100g (3½oz) caster sugar

3 medium eggs, lightly beaten

1 tsp vanilla extract

40g (1½oz) plain flour

6 large filo pastry sheets

icing sugar to dust

cream, vanilla ice cream or
  crème fraîche to serve

1 Melt the chocolate in a heatproof
   bowl over a pan of gently simmering
   water (make sure the base of the bowl
   doesn't touch the water). When melted
   and smooth, put the chocolate to one
   side to cool for 15 minutes.

2 Put 40g (1½oz) of the butter and all
   the caster sugar into a separate large
   bowl and beat together with a hand-
   held electric whisk until pale and
   fluffy. Gradually add the eggs, beating
   well after each addition. Next beat in
   the vanilla, then fold in the flour with a
   large metal spoon. Finally, fold in the

melted and cooled chocolate. Chill the
mixture until firm, about 1 hour.

3 When the chocolate mixture is firm,
   melt the remaining butter. Trim all the
   filo sheets into rough 30.5 × 30.5cm
   (12 × 12in) squares. Lay out four of
   the filo squares, then brush each
   with melted butter. Top each with
   another filo square and brush again
   with butter. Next, using your hands,
   shape a quarter of the firm chocolate
   mixture into a ball (it will be messy!)
   and put in the middle of one of the
   squares. Repeat with the remaining
   chocolate mixture. Wash your hands
   before gathering the pastry above the
   filling, squeezing tightly to seal and
   scrunching lightly on top. Transfer to
   a baking tray. Repeat with remaining
   parcels. Chill for 30 minutes.

4 Preheat the oven to 180°C (160°C fan
   oven) mark 4 and bake the parcels for
   15 minutes. Dust with icing sugar and
   serve immediately with cream, vanilla
   ice cream or crème fraîche.

SAVE EFFORT

Prepare to the end of step 2 up to
6 hours ahead. Complete to the
end of step 3 up to 2 hours ahead.
Complete the recipe to serve.

Serves 4

Brandy Snaps

Hands-on time: 10 minutes
Cooking time: 12 minutes, plus cooling

50g (2oz) butter, plus extra to grease

50g (2oz) caster sugar

2 tbsp golden syrup

50g (2oz) plain flour

½ tsp ground ginger

1 tsp brandy

finely grated zest of ½ lemon

150ml (¼ pint) double cream

1 Preheat the oven to 180°C (160°C fan oven) mark 4. Line two or three large baking sheets with baking parchment.

2 Gently heat the butter, sugar and syrup in a pan until the butter has melted and the sugar has dissolved. Remove from the heat.

3 Sift the flour and ginger together, then stir into the melted mixture with the brandy and lemon zest.

4 Drop teaspoonfuls of the mixture on to the prepared baking sheets, leaving 10cm (4in) between each one. Bake for 7 minutes or until cooked

5 Using a palette knife, quickly remove from the baking sheets and roll each one around the buttered handle of a wooden spoon. Leave on the handles until set, then gently twist to remove. Cool on a wire rack.

6 If the biscuits set before they have been shaped, return them to the oven for a few minutes to soften. Store in an airtight container until required.

7 Just before serving, whip the cream until it just holds its shape. Spoon into a piping bag fitted with a star nozzle and pipe cream into the brandy snaps. Serve immediately.

Makes about 12

Pumpkin Seed Brittle

🍴 **Hands-on time:** 5 minutes
Cooking time: about 12 minutes

100g (3½oz) caster sugar
40g (1½oz) pumpkin seeds

SAVE EFFORT

Make the brittle, but don't break,
up to 1 hour ahead.

1 Put the caster sugar into a pan and add 75ml (3fl oz) water. Heat gently, stirring to dissolve the sugar, then turn up the heat and cook without stirring until the sugar turns a deep caramel colour – swirl the pan occasionally.

2 While the sugar is cooking, line a large baking sheet with baking parchment. Pour the caramel on to the prepared sheet, spreading to a thin, even layer with a spatula.

3 Sprinkle the pumpkin seeds over and press in lightly with the spatula. Leave to harden. Bash into shards with a rolling pin and serve with coffee.

Serves 12

Luscious Lemon Passion Pots

Hands-on time: 5 minutes, plus chilling (optional)

150g (5oz) condensed milk

50ml (2fl oz) double cream

grated zest and juice of 1 large lemon

1 passion fruit

1 Put the condensed milk, double cream and lemon zest and juice into a medium bowl and whisk until thick and fluffy. Spoon into two small ramekins or coffee cups and chill until needed – or carry on with the recipe if you can't wait.

2 To serve, halve the passion fruit, scoop out the seeds and use to decorate the lemon pots.

Perfect Chocolate

Chocolate is a delicious dessert ingredient. It also makes great decorations, and a simple sauce with many variations. The type of chocolate you choose will have a dramatic effect on the end product. For the best results, buy chocolate that has a high proportion of cocoa solids, preferably at least 70%.

Chocolate shavings

This is the easiest decoration of all because it doesn't call for melting chocolate. Use chilled chocolate.

1 Hold a chocolate bar upright on a worksurface and shave pieces off the edge with a Y-shaped vegetable peeler.

2 Alternatively, grate the chocolate against a coarse or medium-coarse grater to make very fine shavings.

Melting

For cooking or making decorations, chocolate is usually melted first.

1 Break the chocolate into pieces and put in a heatproof bowl or in the top of a double boiler. Set over a pan of gently simmering water.

2 Heat very gently until the chocolate starts to melt, then stir only once or twice until completely melted.

Larger chocolate curls

1 Spread melted chocolate in a thin layer on a marble slab, baking sheet or clean worksurface. Leave to firm up.
2 Using a sharp, flat-ended blade (such as a metal pastry scraper), push through the chocolate at a 45-degree angle. The size of the curls will be determined by the width of the blade.

Chocolate sauce

1 Chop plain chocolate (at least 70% cocoa solids) and put it in a saucepan with 50ml (2fl oz) water per 100g (3½oz) chocolate.
2 Heat slowly, allowing the chocolate to melt, then stir until the sauce is smooth.

Chocolate Truffle Espresso Tart

Hands-on time: 30 minutes, plus chilling
Cooking time: about 30 minutes

For the pastry

175g (6oz) plain flour, plus extra to dust
80g (3oz) icing sugar, sifted
100g (3½oz) chilled butter,
  cut into cubes
1 large egg yolk
1 tsp vanilla extract

For the filling

1 tbsp instant coffee
300ml (½ pint) double cream
25g (1oz) golden syrup
50g (2oz) butter
75g (3oz) each plain chocolate and milk
  chocolate, very finely chopped

To decorate

150g (5oz) plain chocolate
icing sugar to dust

1 To make the pastry, put the flour and
  icing sugar into a food processor and
  pulse briefly to mix. Add the butter
  and pulse until the mixture resembles
  fine breadcrumbs (alternatively, rub

the butter into the mixture using your
fingers). Add the egg yolk and vanilla
and pulse again until the pastry just
comes together (add a tsp or two of
water if the mixture looks dry). Tip on
to a lightly floured worksurface, press
gently together to form a disc, then
wrap in clingfilm. Chill for 30 minutes
or until firm but pliable.

2 Preheat the oven to 180°C (160°C fan
  oven) mark 4. Roll the pastry out on a
  lightly floured worksurface, then use
  to line a 20.5cm (8in) round, 2.5cm
  (1in) deep fluted flan tin and prick the
  base all over with a fork. Put the tin on
  a baking tray and chill for 10 minutes.

3 When chilled, cover the pastry with a
  sheet of greaseproof paper and fill
  (on top of the greaseproof) with
  baking beans. Bake for 20 minutes,
  then lift out the beans and paper. Put
  the pastry tin back into the oven and
  bake for 8–10 minutes more until the
  pastry is golden and feels sandy to
  the touch.

4 Meanwhile, make the filling. In a medium pan, stir together the coffee granules and 1 tbsp boiling water, then add the cream and golden syrup. Bring the mixture to the boil, stirring occasionally, then turn off the heat and immediately stir in the butter and both types of chocolate until smooth (if they don't melt completely, heat very gently, stirring constantly, until they do). Pour the filling into the pastry case (still in its tin) and chill for at least 4 hours or overnight.

5 Meanwhile, melt the 150g (5oz) plain chocolate in a heatproof bowl over a pan of gently simmering water (make sure the base of the bowl doesn't touch the water). When melted and smooth, pour on to a flat baking sheet. Chill for 10 minutes until just set but not solid. Pull a large knife towards you across the chocolate to make a curl. Repeat until you have enough curls to cover the top of the tart, then dust with icing sugar and serve the tart in slices.

SAVE TIME

Complete the tart up to a day ahead. Remove from the fridge 10 minutes before serving.

Serves 10

Rose Chocolates

Hands-on time: 10 minutes, plus freezing
Cooking time: about 1 minute

50g (2oz) white chocolate, chopped
50g (2oz) milk chocolate, chopped
50g (2oz) plain chocolate, chopped
a selection of sprinkles, coloured sugar,
   gold leaf and sugar roses to decorate

1 Put each type of chocolate into a small, microwave-safe bowl. Put the bowls side by side in the microwave and heat on full power for 1 minute. Continue heating for 10 second bursts until the chocolates are melted and smooth (you may need to take them out at different times).

2 Meanwhile, line two baking sheets with baking parchment. Drop scant teaspoonfuls of the different types of melted chocolate on to the prepared sheets, spacing a little apart, then smooth into rounds with the back of a teaspoon.

3 Decorate the chocolates with sprinkles, coloured sugar, gold leaf or sugar roses. Freeze for 10 minutes to set, then pack into a tissue-lined box and give with love. Serve with coffee.

Makes about 36

Fig, Honey and Marsala Tart

Hands-on time: 15 minutes, plus chilling
Cooking time: about 25 minutes, plus cooling

375g (13oz) shortcrust pastry

plain flour to dust

250g (9oz) full-fat mascarpone

400ml (14fl oz) double cream

50ml (2fl oz) Marsala dessert wine

75g (3oz) icing sugar

8 fresh figs, quartered

200g (7oz) raspberries

25g (1oz) pistachio nuts, roughly chopped

1–2 tbsp clear honey

SAVE TIME

Blind-bake the pastry up to a day ahead. Leave to cool completely, then loosely cover with foil. Complete the recipe to serve. Use a ready-baked tart case to speed up this recipe even more.

1 Preheat the oven to 220°C (200°C fan oven) mark 7. Roll out the pastry on a lightly floured worksurface and use to line a 4cm (1½in) deep, 20.5cm (8in) round loose-bottomed fluted tart tin. Chill the lined tin in the freezer for 5 minutes.

2 Put the tin on a baking sheet and line pastry with baking parchment. Fill with baking beans or uncooked rice and bake for 15 minutes. Remove the beans/rice and paper and bake for a further 5–10 minutes until the base is cooked through and feels sandy to the touch. Remove from the oven and leave to cool completely.

3 Put the mascarpone, cream and Marsala into a bowl and sift over the icing sugar. Whisk until thick.

4 Take the cooled tart case out of the tin and transfer it to a serving plate. Fill with the mascarpone mixture and arrange the fruit on top. Sprinkle the pistachios over and drizzle over the honey. Serve in slices.

Serves 8

White Chocolate and Pistachio Profiteroles

Hands-on time: 30 minutes
Cooking time: about 30 minutes, plus cooling

60g (2½oz) butter, cubed, plus extra to grease

75g (3oz) plain flour

2 medium eggs, well beaten

50g (2oz) pistachios

75g (3oz) white chocolate, chopped

450ml (¾ pint) double cream

3 tbsp icing sugar

1 Put the butter and 125ml (4fl oz) water into a large pan. Gently heat to melt the butter, then bring to the boil. Take off the heat, then quickly whisk in the flour. Carry on whisking until the mixture comes away from the sides of the pan (about 30 seconds). Cool for 15 minutes.

2 Preheat the oven to 200°C (180°C fan oven) mark 6 and lightly grease two baking sheets. Gradually whisk the eggs into the pan containing the cooled flour mixture, beating after each addition. Dollop teaspoonfuls of mixture on the baking sheets, spacing them well apart (you should have about 24). Use a damp finger to smooth the tops, then bake for about 25 minutes or until puffed and a deep golden colour.

3 Take out of the oven and pierce a hole in the bottom of each profiterole with a metal skewer – this will allow steam to escape. Transfer to a wire rack and leave to cool completely.

4 Meanwhile, put the pistachios into a food processor and whiz until finely ground. Put to one side. Melt half the white chocolate in a heatproof bowl over a pan of gently simmering water (make sure the base of the bowl doesn't touch the water). Leave to cool for about 10 minutes.

5 Put the cream and icing sugar into a large bowl and whip until the mixture holds soft peaks. Whisk in half the ground pistachios and the cooled

Makes 8

melted chocolate. Insert a 5mm (¼in) nozzle into a piping bag, then fill the bag with the cream and pipe into the cooled profiteroles via the steam hole.

6 Stack the profiteroles on a serving plate. Melt the remaining white chocolate as before, then drizzle over the profiteroles. Scatter the remaining pistachios over them and serve.

SAVE TIME

For convenience, complete the recipe to the end of step 5 up to one day in advance, then chill. Complete the recipe up to 3 hours ahead and chill until ready to serve.

White Chocolate and Basil Mousse

Hands-on time: 15 minutes, plus freezing
Cooking time: about 10 minutes

4 gelatine leaves, each measuring
 11½ × 6½cm (4½ × 2½in), broken
 into small pieces

300ml (½ pint) double cream

150g (5oz) white chocolate,
 finely chopped

20g fresh basil leaves, plus extra small
 leaves to decorate

2 medium eggs

50g (2oz) caster sugar

cocoa powder to dust

Brandy Snaps (see page 150) to serve

1 Put the gelatine leaves into a bowl
 and cover with 75ml (3fl oz) boiling
 water. Stir until the gelatine completely
 dissolves. Next, put the double cream,
 white chocolate and basil into a pan
 and gently heat, stirring occasionally,
 until the chocolate melts. Take off the
 heat and leave the mixture to infuse for
 about 10 minutes.

2 In a separate bowl, whisk together the
 eggs and sugar with an electric hand
 whisk until thick and moussey, about 5

minutes – when you move the beaters
through the mixture, they should leave
a trail that's visible for a few seconds.

3 Strain the basil mixture into the egg
 bowl, then pour in the gelatine water.
 Beat quickly to combine, then divide
 the mixture among six glasses. Freeze
 for about 45 minutes, then transfer
 to the fridge until needed. Dust each
 mousse lightly with cocoa powder,
 decorate with basil and serve with
 Brandy Snaps or a similar crunchy
 biscuit, if you like.

Note: As this pudding contains raw eggs,
buy those with the British Lion mark and
don't serve to vulnerable groups.

SAVE TIME

Make mousses up to a day ahead
chill overnight (no need to freeze),
then complete the recipe to serve.

Serves 6

Perfect Coffee and Tea

Use this handy guide to help you find out how
much coffee and tea to serve at your event.

Coffee and tea	
Ground coffee	125g (4oz) for 12 medium cups
Instant	75g (3oz) for 12 large cups
Milk	allow 450ml (¾ pint) for 12 cups of tea

Approximate coffee and tea quantities

COFFEE GROUND

1 serving	200ml (7fl oz)
24-26 servings	250–275g (9–10oz) coffee
If you make the coffee in advance, strain it after infusion.	3.4 litres (6 pints) water
Reheat without boiling.	1.7 litres (3 pints) milk
	450g (1lb) sugar

Tea

INDIAN

1 serving	200ml (7fl oz)
24-26 servings	50g (2oz) tea
It is better to make tea in several pots rather	4.5 litres (8 pints) water
than in one outsized one.	900ml (1½ pints) milk
	450g (1lb) sugar

CHINA

1 serving	200ml (7fl oz)
24-26 servings	50g (2oz) tea
Infuse China tea for 2–3 minutes only.	5.1 litres (9 pints) water
Put a thin lemon slice in each cup before pouring.	2–3 lemons
Serve sugar separately.	450g (1lb) sugar

Irish or Gaelic Coffee

To serve one, you will need:
25ml (1fl oz) Irish whiskey, 1 tsp
brown sugar, 85–125ml (3–4fl oz) hot
double-strength black coffee
1–2 tbsp double cream, chilled.

1 Gently warm a glass, pour in the
   whiskey and add the brown sugar.
2 Pour in the black coffee to within
   2.5cm (1in) of the brim and stir
   to dissolve the sugar.
3 Fill to the brim with cream, poured
   over the back of a spoon, and leave
   to stand for a few minutes.

Liqueur coffee around the world

The following are made as for Irish
Coffee. Allow 25ml (1fl oz) of the
liqueur or spirit to 125ml (4fl oz) of
double-strength black coffee, with
sugar to taste – usually about 1 tsp –
and some thick double cream to pour
on top; these quantities will make
1 glassful:

❑ Cointreau Coffee
   (made with Cointreau)
❑ Caribbean Coffee
   (made with rum)
❑ German Coffee
   (made with Kirsch)
❑ Normandy Coffee
   (made with Calvados)
❑ Russian Coffee
   (made with vodka)
❑ Calypso Coffee
   (made with Tia Maria)
❑ Witch's Coffee
   (made with strega; sprinkle a
   little grated lemon zest on top)
❑ Curaçao Coffee
   (made with curaçao; stir with
   a stick of cinnamon)

Per half egg: 124 cal
6g protein ♥ 9g fat (2g sat)
0.3g fibre ♥ 6g carb
0.6g salt

14

Per canapé: 43 cal
3g protein ♥ 2g fat (1g sat)
0.2g fibre ♥ 3g carb
0.2g salt

16

50 cal ♥ 0.7g protein
3g fat (1g sat) ♥ 0.8g fibre
4g carb ♥ 0.2g salt

18

Per canapé : 132 cal
3g protein ♥ 9g fat (3g sa
0.5g fibre ♥ 11g carb
0.5g salt

22

114 cal ♥ 0g protein
0g fat ♥ 0g fibre
10g carb ♥ 0g salt

32

Per serving: 83 cal
0g protein ♥ 0g fat (0g sat)
0g fibre ♥ 7g carb ♥ 0g salt

34

134 cal ♥ 0g protein
0g fat ♥ 0g fibre
16g carb ♥ 0g salt

36

90 cal ♥ 4g protein
6g fat (1g sat) ♥ 2g fibre
8g carb ♥ 0.3g salt

50

Per serving: 129 cal
4g protein ♥ 9g fat (6g sat)
2g fibre ♥ 8g carb ♥ 0.5g salt

52

Per pitta: 159 cal ♥ 5g pro
1g fat (0.2g sat) ♥ 1g fib
34g carb ♥ 0.3g salt

54

162 cal ♥ 3g protein
6g fat (1g sat) ♥ 2g fibre
27g carb ♥ 0.1g salt

68

139 cal ♥ 3g protein
2g fat (1g sat) ♥ 2g fibre
30g carb ♥ 0.5g salt

70

74 cal ♥ 0.8g protein
5g fat (2g sat) ♥ 2g fibre
6g carb ♥ 0.5g salt

72

36 cal ♥ 0.7g protein
3g fat (0.5g sat) ♥ 1g fibr
3g carb ♥ 0g salt

74

Calorie Gallery

56 cal ♥ 2g protein
g fat (2g sat) ♥ 0.1g fibre
3g carb ♥ 0.2g salt

4

Per canapé: 36 cal
1g protein ♥ 4g fat (0.5g sat)
0.1g fibre ♥ 1g carb ♥ 0.3g salt

26

Per blini: 43 cal ♥ 2g protein
3g fat (1g sat) ♥ 0.1g fibre
2g carb ♥ 0.3g salt

28

Per canapé: 47 cal
7g protein ♥ 1 fat (0.3g sat)
0g fibre ♥ 3g carb ♥ 0.1g salt

30

Without cream:
73 cal ♥ 2g protein
0g fat ♥ 0.8g fibre
18g carb ♥ 0g salt

112 cal ♥ 0.2g protein
0g fat ♥ 0g fibre
15g carb ♥ 0g salt

44

(B) Per serving: 38 cal
0.3g protein ♥ 0g fat (0g sat)
0.2g fibre ♥ 8g carb ♥ 0g salt

(L) Per serving: 121 cal
0.4g protein ♥ 6g fat (1g sat)
0.3g fibre ♥ 17g carb ♥ 1.0g salt

(R) Per serving: 57 cal
0.6g protein ♥ 6g fat (1g sat)
0.1g fibre ♥ 1g carb ♥ 2.5g salt

46

174 cal ♥ 14g protein
12g fat (3g sat) ♥ 2g fibre
2g carb ♥ 0.2g salt

440 cal ♥ 14g protein
36g fat (29g sat) ♥ 0.7g fibre
17g carb ♥ 1.8g salt

60

457 cal ♥ 23g protein
34g fat (17g sat) ♥ 2g fibre
17g carb ♥ 2.7g salt

64

321 cal ♥ 12g protein
31g fat (15g sat) ♥ 0.3g fibre
1g carb ♥ 0.8g salt

66

30 cal ♥ 1g protein
g fat (trace sat) ♥ 2g fibre
3g carb ♥ 0g salt

127 cal ♥ 7g protein
11g fat (2g sat) ♥ 2g fibre
1g carb ♥ 0.1g salt

80

98 cal ♥ 3g protein
5g fat (2g sat) ♥ 1g fibre
11g carb ♥ 0.2g salt

82

370 cal ♥ 27g protein
28g fat (18g sat) ♥ 0g fibre
<0.1g carb ♥ 1.9g salt

84

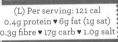

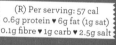

336 cal ♥ 13g protein
14g fat (6g sat) ♥ 4g fibre
37g carb ♥ 1.8g salt

86

180 cal ♥ 13g protein
9g fat (3g sat) ♥ 7g fibre
14g carb ♥ 1.3g salt

88

503 cal ♥ 62g protein
19g fat (8g sat) ♥ 0.4g fibre
14g carb ♥ 3.8g salt

92

173 cal ♥ 21g protein
9g fat (3g sat) ♥ 0g fibre
3g carb ♥ 1.1g salt

96

205 cal ♥ 10g protein
3g fat (2g sat) ♥ 2g fibre
36g carb ♥ 0.3g salt

108

737 cal ♥ 37g protein
65g fat (40g sat) ♥ 0g fibre
2g carb ♥ 1.7g salt

110

149 cal ♥ 34g protein
1g fat (0g sat) ♥ 0g fibre
0g carb ♥ 0.3g salt

112

499 cal ♥ 44g protein
13g fat (6g sat) ♥ 3g fibre
50g carb ♥ 1.3g salt

114

Per serving (for 6): 757 cal
55g protein ♥ 62g fat (25g sat)
0.2g fibre ♥ 7g carb ♥ 0.5g salt
Per serving (for 8): 568 cal
41g protein ♥ 47g fat (19g sat)
0.1g fibre ♥ 5g carb ♥ 0.5g salt

124

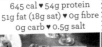

645 cal ♥ 54g protein
51g fat (18g sat) ♥ 0g fibre
0g carb ♥ 0.5g salt

126

502 calories ♥ 41g protein
23g fat (8g sat) ♥ 2g fibre
14g carb ♥ 0.7g salt

128

614 cal ♥ 7g protein
43g fat (23g sat) ♥ 0.3g fibre
45g carb ♥ 0.9g salt

138

Per brandy snap: 137 cal
0.6g protein ♥ 10g fat (6g sat)
0.1g fibre ♥ 11g carb ♥ 0.1g salt

150

52 cal ♥ 2g protein
2g fat (0.2g sat) ♥ 0.4g fibre
9g carb ♥ 0g salt

152

377 cal ♥ 7g protein
21g fat (13g sat) ♥ 0.3g fibre
43g carb ♥ 0.3g salt

154

473 cal ♥ 4g protein
35g fat (22g sat) ♥ 1.1g fibre
37g carb ♥ 0.1g salt

158

69 cal ♥ 10g protein
g fat (21g sat) ♥ 3g fibre
36g carb ♥ 1.0g salt

477 cal ♥ 8g protein
28g fat (19g sat) ♥ 4g fibre
50g carb ♥ 0.8g salt

113 cal ♥ 12g protein
6g fat (1g sat) ♥ 0g fibre
1g carb ♥ 0.1g salt

683 cal ♥ 12g protein
57g fat (27g sat) ♥ 2g fibre
33g carb ♥ 1.5g salt

93 cal ♥ 31g protein
fat (12g sat) ♥ 0.3g fibre
0g carb ♥ 0.4g salt

583 cal ♥ 34g protein
30g fat (15g sat) ♥ 4g fibre
45g carb ♥ 1.2g salt

384 cal ♥ 43g protein
17g fat (6g sat) ♥ 1g fibre
9g carb ♥ 0.8g salt

383 cal ♥ 36g protein
23g fat (10g sat) ♥ 0.9g fibre
23g carb ♥ 1.0g salt

433 cal ♥ 4g protein
8g fat (14g sat) ♥ 1g fibre
55g carb ♥ 0.1g salt

702 cal ♥ 7g protein
51g fat (30g sat) ♥ 1g fibre
58g carb ♥ 0.8g salt

383 cal ♥ 2g protein
27g fat (16g sat) ♥ 0.7g fibre
31g carb ♥ 0.1g salt

Per serving: 782 cal
11g protein ♥ 37g fat (20g sat)
2.0g fibre ♥ 109g carb
0.4g salt

Per chocolate: 22 cal
.3g protein ♥ 1.2g fat
(0.7g sat) ♥ 0.1g fibre
3g carb ♥ 0g salt

682 cal ♥ 6g protein
55g fat (34g sat) ♥ 3g fibre
41g carb ♥ 0.8g salt

Per profiterole:
496 cal ♥ 5g protein
44g fat (25g sat) ♥ 0.7g fibre
20g carb ♥ 0.3g salt

444 cal ♥ 7g protein
37g fat (22g sat) ♥ 0g fibre
24g carb ♥ 0.2g salt

Index

PICTURE CREDITS
Photographers:
Neil Barclay (page 65);
Martin Brigdale (page 77);
Nicki Dowey (pages 11, 33, 35,
37, 61 and 81); Will Heap
(page 13); Fiona Kennedy (page
151); Gareth Morgans (pages 43,
46, 51, 53, 101, 103, 105, 113, 125,
129, 149, 153 and 163); Myles New
(pages 17, 19, 23, 25, 27, 31, 45, 59,
67, 71, 87, 107, 117, 119, 121, 139, 143
and 145); Craig Robertson (pages
56, 62, 90, 91, 93, 94, 95, 141, 156
and 157); Sam Stowell (page 15);
Lucinda Symons (pages 29 and
55); Kate Whitaker (pages 69, 73,
75, 83, 85, 89, 97, 109, 111, 115, 123,
127, 147, 155, 159, 161, 165 and 167).

Home Economists:
Joanna Farrow, Emma Jane
Frost, Teresa Goldfinch, Alice
Hart, Lucy McKelvie, Kim
Morphew, Aya Nishimura,
Katie Rogers, Bridget Sargeson,
Kate Trend and Mari Mererid
Williams.

Stylists: Tamzin Ferdinando,
Wei Tang, Helen Trent and
Fanny Ward.

BAKE ME A CAKE
There's always time for cake

EASY PEASY MEALS
Easy meals for every day

LET'S DO BRUNCH
Mouth-watering meals to start your day

CHEAP EATS
Budget-busting ideas that won't break the bank

SALAD DAYS
Oh-so-fresh ideas for fabulous salads

Available online at store.anovabooks.com and from all good bookshops

POSH NOSH
Delicious recipes to impress your guests

PARTY FOOD
Delicious recipes to get the party started

SLOW STOPPERS
Slow-cooked meals packed with flavour

GREAT VEG
Inspired ideas for delicious veggie meals

AL FRESCO EATS
Easy grills, barbecues and picnics

ROAST IT
There's nothing better than a delicious roast

FLASH IN THE PAN
Spice up your noodles and stir-fries

GLUTEN-FREE AND EASY
Oh-so-good-for-you recipes that taste great

LOW FAT LOW CAL
Nice recipes don't need to be naughty